WAITING FOR THE WORD

WAITING FOR THE WORD

Dietrich Bonhoeffer on Speaking about God

FRITS DE LANGE

Translated by

Martin N. Walton

WILLIAM B. EERDMANS PUBLISHING COMPANY

GRAND RAPIDS, MICHIGAN / CAMBRIDGE, U.K.

© 1995 Ten Have b.v., Baarn, the Netherlands
Originally published in Dutch as.
Wachten op het verlossende woord: Dietrich Bonhoeffer en het spreken over God

English translation © 2000 Wm. B. Eerdmans Publishing Co.
255 Jefferson Ave. S.E., Grand Rapids, Michigan 49503 /
P.O. Box 163, Cambridge CB3 9PU U.K.

Printed in the United States of America

05 04 03 02 01 00   7 6 5 4 3 2 1

Library of Congress Cataloging-in-Publication Data

Lange, Frederik de, 1955-
    [Wachten op het verlossende woord. English]
    Waiting for the word: Dietrich Bonhoeffer on speaking about God / Frits de Lange;
translated by Martin N. Walton
        p.   cm.
    Includes bibliographical references.
    ISBN 0-8028-4532-0 (pbk.: alk. paper)
    1. Bonhoeffer, Dietrich, 1906-1945 — Contributions in doctrine of knowableness of
God. 2. God — Knowableness — History of doctrines — 20th century. I. Title.

BT98.B66 L2612 2000
231'.092 — dc21   99-49037

Contents

1 Silence on God?

An Exploration

In the more than fifty years that have passed since April 9, 1945, the day that Dietrich Bonhoeffer, the German theologian and member of the German Resistance Movement against Hitler, was hanged in the concentration camp of Flossenburg, he has become a companion and conversation partner for many in the world of church and theology. Despite the fact that he only reached the age of 39, he has accompanied an entire generation that sought a faithful response to the challenges of postwar Western society. In a rapidly secularizing society Bonhoeffer's words, formulated in his letters from prison, about a world come of age and about a nonreligious interpretation of biblical concepts were a welcome stimulus and guidepost. The so-called secularization theology of the 1950s and 1960s (represented by Paul M. van Buren and John A. T. Robinson, among others) carried the conviction that it was a continuation of Bonhoeffer's thoughts. They believed that they could connect the dotted lines that Bonhoeffer had only fragmentarily sketched in his letters. They considered Bonhoeffer to be a vivid conversation partner in theological dialogue who represented an established position in the debate with Paul Tillich, Rudolf Bultmann, and Karl Barth.

In a world likewise subject to globalization and worldwide developments, Bonhoeffer's words about a church for others that viewed the world from the perspective of the suffering and oppressed, the "view from below" (*LPP*, 17), served as an eye-opener. The liberation theologians of the 1960s and 1970s (Gustavo Gutiérrez, Hugo Assmann, Leonardo Boff, and others) found in Bonhoeffer a European ally of their format who had not only provided a theological theory for situations of political suffering and oppression but had also put it into practice. Had he not himself exemplified how a theology of praxis could be born? From South Africa to East Germany, from Brazil to Japan, Bonhoeffer proved to be an inspiring contemporary, despite (or perhaps due to) the fact that he was killed as a martyr for the sake of Christ. Even if his voice had been silenced, in theology his words have remained formidable.

1.1 Bonhoeffer as Conversation Partner

Half a century is, however, a long time. The chasm between Bonhoeffer and us has become so great that it seems unbridgeable. His name sounds less and less in theological conversation. In religious education he, along with Martin Luther King and Albert Schweitzer, is perhaps still pointed to as a believer who stood for what he said. But what he said is for many students more than they can intellectually digest.

The theology of Bonhoeffer seems to have lost a good deal of its popularity. Whereas in the 1950s and 1960s he was a paragon of theological progressiveness, some now reproach him for his elitist conservatism.[1] The judgment is that if Bonhoeffer is considered a partisan of those who are downtrodden, then he has only been half read. Did he not as an antidemocrat defend in his *Ethics* an authoritarian ethic of "above and below"? His criticism was apparently not directed at social hierarchy as such, but at the fact that the hierarchy had been turned upside down by Nazism. Those who sat in power above belonged below, and vice versa.

Not only his ethics but also his dogmatics seems to frustrate rather than stimulate contemporary theological discussion. Matters that are now at the top of the agenda were for Bonhoeffer a half century ago not a top priority. A Christian who now seeks to pursue dialogue with other religions will not likely begin with the exclusiveness of Christ nor seek a foundation for theology in an exclusive christocentric model. Bonhoeffer did just that, although one should remember that he was not engaged in dialogue with other religions but in conflict with Fascists. Nevertheless, for Bonhoeffer, it was Christ from beginning to end. He is not to be re-

---

1. Cf. K.-M. Kodalle, *Dietrich Bonhoeffer — Zur Kritik seiner Theologie* (Dietrich Bonhoeffer — a critique of his theology) (Gütersloh: Gütersloher Verlag, 1991).

proached for that. But how is one now to approach a Hindu or Muslim from that standpoint? His concentration on Christology has in the meantime gained him a warm reception by groups that previously avoided him. In orthodox Protestant circles there are those who attempt to bring the "other Bonhoeffer" to the limelight. Bonhoeffer even loses his "odium" of theological progressiveness and is presented as a "church father" of evangelicals (Georg Huntemann).[2] One could ask: Is this "other" Bonhoeffer, pious and conservative as he is, the real Bonhoeffer?

In Bonhoeffer's work one can also hardly find building blocks for a theology of nature, which is now important.[3] Nor does his thought lend itself to the purposes of feminist theology.[4] Bonhoeffer based his thought on Christ, not on creation, and he maintained quite conservative viewpoints on the role of women. One also seeks in vain any points of contact in Bonhoeffer's writings with new forms of spirituality that go under the name of "New Age." "People as they are now simply cannot be religious any more," he wrote from his prison cell on April 30, 1944 (*LPP,* 279). In view of the present unbridled growth of religious movements, one can only conclude that Bonhoeffer was mistaken.

Is Bonhoeffer the theologian a fellow traveler, a partner in conversation, or even a man ahead of his times? Perhaps he was all these from the 1950s into the 1970s, but, at least according to some, he is no longer relevant in the 1990s. Bonhoeffer seems to have finally fallen on the fields of history, with honor to be sure, but he seems nevertheless to miss contact with current theological discourses. No one would deny him a place of honor among the great ones of theology, but it is perhaps time that he be moved to a different level of significance. He seems gradually to become more at home in modern church history than in systematic theology.[5]

2. Georg Huntemann, *The Other Bonhoeffer: An Evangelical Reassessment,* trans. Todd Huizenga (Grand Rapids: Baker, 1993).

3. Cf., however, Larry R. Rasmussen, *Earth Community, Earth Ethics* (Maryknoll, N.Y.: Orbis, 1996), 295-316.

4. Cf. Helga Kuhlmann, "Die Ethik Dietrich Bonhoeffers — Quelle oder Hemmschuh für feministisch-theologische Ethik?" (Dietrich Bonhoeffer's ethics: Source or hindrance for feminist-theological ethics?), *Zeitschrift für Evangelische Ethik* 37/2 (1993) 106-20.

5. The number of attempts to actualize Bonhoeffer's theology is decreasing, at least in Europe, whereas the number of historical studies is growing (in quality as well). Examples of the latter are Christoph Strohm, *Theologische Ethik im Kampf gegen den National- sozialismus: Der Weg Dietrich Bonhoeffers mit den Juristen Hans von Dohnanyi und*

How should the fiftieth anniversary of Bonhoeffer's death be commemorated other than with a fitting homage to a courageous man? Perhaps it would be better to leave the man's theology for what it is and direct attention to his piety or resistance activities. Nonetheless, this book wants to focus on Bonhoeffer as a theologian, in the broad, literal sense of the word: "one who speaks about God." He was just that, as is every believer more or less. But besides being a Christian and a churchman Bonhoeffer was also a theologian in a more specific sense, as one who tried to speak about God in a responsible manner, in dialogue with contemporary culture and in response to Christian tradition, and as one who dedicated his life to that task. This book seeks only to provide a small reconstruction of that attempt.

It is not my intention to provide an outline of Bonhoeffer's entire theology. I set clear limits: I examine Bonhoeffer with regard to his speaking about God, only insofar as he provides an account of that speaking itself. I put to him the question how he considers it possible for people to say something sensible about God and in which language that would have to be done. In other words, according to him, what are the conditions, but also the possibilities and limits, of speaking meaningfully about God?

1.2 The Speechlessness of Church and Theology

Four considerations constitute the background for this question.

a. We confront here the central question of all theology, not just Christian theology: Can anything be sensibly asserted about God? "We are speaking about God. It shouldn't surprise you if you do not comprehend it! If you

---

Gerhard Leibholz in den Widerstand (Theological ethics in the struggle against National Socialism: Dietrich Bonhoeffer's way with the jurists Hans von Dohnanyi and Gerhard Leibholz in the Resistance Movement) (Munich: Chr. Kaiser, 1989); and Christine-Ruth Müller, *Dietrich Bonhoeffers Kampf gegen die nationalsozialistische Verfolgung und Vernichtung der Juden: Bonhoeffers Haltung zur Judenfrage im Vergleich mit Stellungnahmen aus der evangelischen Kirche und Kreisen des deutschen Widerstandes* (Dietrich Bonhoeffer's struggle against the National Socialist persecution and extermination of the Jews: Bonhoeffer's attitude toward the Jewish question in comparison with positions in the Evangelical Church and circles of the German Resistance Movement) (Munich: Chr. Kaiser, 1990).

were to comprehend him, it would not be God." That is the manner in which Augustine formulated the original dilemma from which theology arises and under which it is at the same time in danger of succumbing: saying something in human language about that which by definition transcends humanity.[6] When one speaks of God, is God not talked to death by the very words that would assert God's living being? "We have to speak about God. However, we are humans and as such we cannot speak about God," according to Karl Barth's version of the same dilemma. His conclusion was emphatically not an advice to keep silent and abandon theology. That would be very impractical, for people would still talk about God, even if theologians no longer allowed it. It is better to ask the question how one might speak *well* about God, "well" in the sense that justice is done to God. That seems an impossible task. As soon as we speak about God, then we are dealing with our ideas on God and not with God himself. And as soon as God would be spoken of directly, then our language would fall short. The paradox of having to speak about God, but not being able to, can only be solved, according to Barth in *The Word of God and the Word of Man* (first published in German in 1924), in the knowledge that only God can speak about God.[7] We will have to learn from God how to speak about God. Our talking about God must emerge from our listening to God. In that way Barth made of the dilemma (*Bedrängnis,* literally "distress") of theology a virtue, namely, its "promise" (*Verheißung*).

The presupposition that God as object can only be spoken of if God as subject wants to speak of himself became an a priori of all theology for Bonhoeffer as a young student. In 1925 he read Barth's book and was so enthusiastic that he remained a resolute, even if critical, ally of Barth's theology. He was an ally not only as a theologian but also as a preacher. In dialectical theology preacher and teacher go closely together. Bonhoeffer defended a theology of the Word that included not only an analysis of speaking about God but also a description of the content and character of God's speaking.

From where did Bonhoeffer derive the courage to do so? Why did he allow himself to be inspired by Barth and not, for example, by a book that had been published three years previously, the *Tractatus Logico-philosoph-*

6. Eberhard Jüngel, *God as the Mystery of the World: On the Foundation of the Theology of the Crucified One in the Dispute between Theism and Atheism,* trans. Darrell L. Guder (Grand Rapids: Eerdmans, 1983), 8.

7. Karl Barth, *The Word of God and the Word of Man,* trans. Douglas Horton (repr., New York: Harper, 1957), 214, 308.

icus by Ludwig Wittgenstein? Even if he never read it, the tenor of the sentence with which it ends must have been familiar to him: "What we cannot speak about, we must pass over in silence."[8] Why did Bonhoeffer not keep his mouth sealed with respect to God? It is worth the trouble to look into his motives.

b. There is an extra reason to look into the matter in our time. In contemporary Western culture hardly anyone loses sleep over the paradoxical precariousness of speaking about God, as indicated by Barth. Speaking about God is not experienced as an impossible possibility but rather as a superfluous exercise. Instead of being a living reality, God seems to have become a commonplace.

Even the curse with which atheists once spoke of God, even if it were only to deny him, has gradually become muted. What remains is the silent shrug of religious indifference — indifference rather than atheism. "God" is in danger of becoming a word without meaning, a symbol lacking vital power.

What can theology do today other than fathom the emptiness that God has left behind, other than say that nothing more can be said of God? *Negative* theology would seem to be the only form of speaking about God that is defensible in our God-forsaken world. One can speak about God only in terms of negation, in terms of what he is *not*. The experience of God's absence is inescapable. The terrors of Hiroshima and Auschwitz indicate the bankruptcy of speaking metaphysically of the positive presence of God. The literary work of Elie Wiesel is exemplary in this respect, marked as it is by the silence of Auschwitz that can only be understood as a silence of God.[9] "Can we still speak about God? Doesn't the failure of modernity imply a failure of that speaking *'about'*?" That is the question asked by the editors of a collection of articles on negative theology. Yes, indeed, is the answer. Negative theology no longer focuses on theology but on the *limits* of theology. "We are no longer able to speak. We can only gropingly put into words the emptiness of not being able to speak."[10]

---

8. Ludwig Wittgenstein, *Tractatus Logico-philosophicus* (1921; repr., London: Routledge & Kegan Paul, 1961), 74.

9. Cf. André Neher, *Exile of the Word: From the Silence of the Bible to the Silence of Auschwitz*, trans. David Maisel (Philadelphia: Jewish Publication Society, 1981).

10. I. N. Bulhof and L. ten Kate, eds., *Ons ontbreken heilige namen: Negatieve theologie in de hedendaagse cultuurfilosofie* (Sacred names are lacking: Negative theology in contemporary philosophy of culture) (Kampen: Kok, 1992), 14, 19.

Even if a half century separates us from Bonhoeffer and he probably never knew the full extent of the terrors of the destruction of the Jews, nevertheless he seems to have had a premonition of the emergence of a cultural climate of religious indifference and the failure of every attempt to turn the tide with words. In one of his letters he attempts to put into words how the question "Who is Christ for us today?" could be answered in a religionless era: "The time when people could be told everything by means of words, whether theological or pious, is over" (*LPP*, 279). Who God is can apparently no longer be *said* to others in modern times.

But must one then remain silent with respect to God? Bonhoeffer placed great value on remaining silent, as we will see. At times he considered it more important than speech. That was true for him in normal human relations but also in relation to God. But he never situated silence in the context of negative theology. Like Eberhard Jüngel he would probably be critical of the pathetic tone that prevails in much contemporary theology with regard to speechlessness.[11] He agreed that in theology one must be able to remain silent, but at the right time and place. In the end Bonhoeffer put silence at the service of a God who has spoken of deity in Jesus Christ. His lectures on Christology in 1933 at the University of Berlin open with the assertion: "Teaching about Christ begins in silence," and he continues: "That has nothing to do with the silence of the mystics, who in their dumbness chatter away secretly in their soul by themselves. The silence of the Church is silence before the Word" (*CC*, 27). That Word is inexpressible, because it has been spoken by none other than God. It is Christ. In a stringent dialectic Bonhoeffer relates speaking and keeping silent to each other. "To speak of Christ means to keep silent; to keep silent about Christ means to speak." Out of that silence Bonhoeffer undertakes a positive unfolding of Christology that can be considered the heart of his theology.[12] Silence constitutes for him the beginning of all theology, but not its end, a condition of its possibility, not the seal of its failure. Apparently we know more about God than only that we know nothing of the deity, thanks to God (see John 1:18b).

The English philosopher of language Ian T. Ramsey has stated that "a

---

11. Jüngel, *God as Mystery*, 4.

12. Cf. H.-J. Abromeit, *Das Geheimnis Christi: Dietrich Bonhoeffers erfahrungs-bezogene Christologie* (The mystery of Christ: Dietrich Bonhoeffer's Christology as related to experience) (Neukirchen: Neukirchener Verlag, 1991), 21-22.

theology that can not be preached is just as objectionable as a proclamation that is not theologically tenable."[13] Bonhoeffer could heartily endorse that. We should ask him how he thinks one can satisfy both conditions, especially because we know that he had a dislike of the massiveness of a "positivism of revelation," of which he encountered only traces in the writings of Barth but which he found so disgusting in the church. Bonhoeffer was not the kind of theologian who overwhelmed with his preaching. "It is only when one knows the unutterability of the name of God that one can utter the name of Jesus Christ" (*LPP,* 157). Bonhoeffer wrote those words in one of his letters from prison in reference to the Old Testament commandment on the name of God. Those who speak with such scruple about God and Christ will not easily raise their voice.

c. It is not just academic theology but also the churches that are currently plagued by embarrassment with regard to how to speak about God. Therein lies another reason to listen again to Bonhoeffer's voice. In 1967 the Dutch theologian of Christian ministry Okke Jager issued an appeal to the churches for the sake of up-to-date proclamation in understandable language. In 1988 at his farewell address he had to admit that "we would do better to recognize in all candor that we no longer know how to speak about God in an understandable manner."[14] In evangelical movements, to be sure, God is still presented in a straightforward way. But the question is if in that way the paradox of Augustine and Barth, the very secret of the living God, is not talked to pieces. Jager attempts to confront the crisis of understanding by means of reflection upon (religious) language. He agrees with Northrop Frye that God is not so much dead as buried in dead language. "Therefore confronting the eclipse of God is first of all a question of language."[15]

---

13. Ian T. Ramsey, *Religious Language: An Empirical Placing of Theological Phrases* (London: SCM, 1957), 180. Cf. 4.5.

14. Okke Jager, *Eigentijdse Verkondiging: Beschouwingen over de vertolking van het Evangelie in het taaleigen van de moderne mens* (Present-day proclamation: Reflections on the interpretation of the gospel in the idiom of modern humanity) (Kampen: Kok, 1967), 21-22; idem, *De verbeelding aan het woord: Pleidooi voor een dichterlijker en zakelijker spreken over God* (Imagination speaks: An argument for speaking more poetically and matter-of-factly about God) (Baarn: Ten Have, 1988), 11.

15. Jager, *Verbeelding,* 146. Cf. Northrop Frye, *The Great Code: Bible and Literature* (New York: Harcourt Brace Jovanovich, 1981).

Jager is not the first person to put it that way. Contemporary theology follows in the wake of the "linguistic turn" that philosophy has made in recent decades. Modern linguistic philosophy no longer considers language to be a representation of reality in our mind, but an instrument by which we can move about in the world. The significations of language are not anchored in an external reality, to which language refers, but in the use we make of language (Wittgenstein).[16] Language becomes a new paradigm for philosophy. Rather than serving as a cement between thought and reality, language itself becomes a location of truth and a creator of reality. Anglo-Saxon theology has pursued in this respect the line of the later Wittgenstein, while the Continental tradition has followed Martin Heidegger and Hans-Georg Gadamer. Various theologians, from Ramsey to Jüngel, have reflected on the consequences of those insights for religious language and attempted to investigate newly discovered dimensions of language (such as metaphor, narrativity, and performative language) for the sake of religion.

Such academic reflection on language, however, seems to rub salt into the wounds of Christian speechlessness rather than help to heal the wounds. The emphasis on the expressive and narrative character of biblical language does not take away the powerlessness of proclamation in the church. "It seems as if the churches have lost their tongues," writes Ernst Lange. "The words with which they are familiar do not change the world. The words that can change the world they are not familiar with."[17] In particular, the churches of the Reformation can take this matter to heart. Did they not arise out of Luther's rediscovery of the liberating power of proclamation, the Word of God as an effective word *(verbum efficax)?* What has happened to preaching that it is no longer a piercing, evocative event, a driving force in time, but only a somnolent monologue?

Bonhoeffer seems to have had a premonition of all this. From his prison cell, in a letter on the occasion of the baptism of his godchild, the son of his niece Renate Schleicher and his friend Eberhard Bethge, he acknowledges that the church is no longer able to speak a reconciling and redeeming word to the world. Its word has become mute and powerless. He

16. Ludwig Wittgenstein, *Philosophical Investigations,* trans. G. E. M. Anscombe (New York: Macmillan, 1958).

17. Ernst Lange, *Chancen des Alltags: Überlegungen zur Funktion des christlichen Gottesdienstes in der Gegenwart* (Everyday chances: Reflections on the function of Christian worship today) (Munich: Chr. Kaiser, 1984), 198.

concludes, "But we are once again being driven back to the beginnings of our understanding" (*LPP*, 299). He points an accusing finger at the church itself. The church is responsible for the fact that its word no longer reaches people. Its life and form are at odds with its proclamation, discrediting it in advance. Later we look more closely at what Bonhoeffer was pointing to (see 2.3 below).

d. Is Bonhoeffer's criticism also applicable to the present-day church? If so, is the church itself solely responsible for the powerlessness of its proclamation? Such a self-accusation would seem to go too far. The written and spoken word as such is subject to devaluation in our culture, a general devaluation that includes words about God as well. The scholarly interest in language seems inversely proportional to the concern for words in society in general, where an image culture seems to supersede a word culture. The churches of the Reformation and their emphasis on the proclamation of the Word seem in this respect to be a relic of a past cultural era. The Bible could excite in the century of Gutenberg, but no longer in that of CNN and MTV. In the eyes of those accustomed to television, of those who are not used to listening, nothing "happens" in a sermon.

Jacques Ellul has related the decrease of numbers in the church directly to "the humiliation of the word" (the title of his book on the matter) in our culture. The triumph of the screen entails a loss of meaning of the written and spoken word. The subtle dialectic of hiddenness and revelation, of presence and absence, of that which is said and that which remains unsaid in the spoken word, makes the word an excellent medium of religious communication. "Only the word can transmit the truth of a religious message," according to the Protestant Ellul.[18] How will truth ever be transmitted in a culture of the viewing screen? In this respect we seem to face the powerlessness of the church rather than its failure.

1.3 A Cautious Way with Words

Bonhoeffer had no part in modern philosophical investigations on language and culture. In his theology one finds no elaborate theory of language, as,

18. Jacques Ellul, *The Humiliation of the Word*, trans. Joyce Main Hanks (Grand Rapids: Eerdmans, 1981), 53.

for example, his contemporary Rosenstock-Huessy developed.[19] Neverthe-less, he would seem capable of contributing to reflection on speaking about God. While recognizing its potential power, Bonhoeffer demon-strated a great sensitivity for the crisis of church proclamation. In addition his posthumously published works exemplify an extraordinary attention to the conditions, the possibilities, and the limits of the spoken word.[20]

19. Cf. W. Rohrbach, *Das Sprachdenken Rosenstock-Huessys* (Rosenstock-Huessy's thoughts on language) (Stuttgart: Kohlhammer, 1973). In *Sanctorum Communio* Bon-hoeffer indicates a line of thought, with reference to Johann Georg Hamann, that he never pursued systematically. He referred there to "the social phenomenon of speech, which is so closely connected with thought that it may well be said that it largely makes thinking possi-ble, and has been given precedence over thought, the word over mind" (*CS*, 46).

20. It is surprising that the topic "Bonhoeffer and religious language" has hardly been systematically researched in Bonhoeffer studies. Despite the fact that his work con-tains various invitations to do so, hardly anyone has considered this to be a topic of itself. Exceptions are perhaps Gerhard Ebeling, "The 'Non-religious Interpretation of Biblical Concepts,'" in idem, *Word and Faith*, trans. James W. Leitch (Philadelphia: Fortress Press, 1963), 98-161 (an essay from 1955); Ernst Feil, *The Theology of Dietrich Bonhoeffer*, trans. Martin Rumscheidt (Philadelphia: Fortress Press, 1985), 46-55; E. G. Wendel, *Studien zur Homiletik Dietrich Bonhoeffers* (Studies on Dietrich Bonhoeffer's homiletics) (Tübingen: Mohr [Siebeck], 1985), 164-65.

One can only guess at the reason for such little attention to the matter. Ebeling was the first who in 1955 dedicated a major and profound essay to Bonhoeffer's later theology and who simultaneously pointed to the problem of language. For a long time he was the only one who did so. His conclusion was that "the problem of non-religious interpretation is . . . decisively concerned with the task of proclamation" (123n.4) The concentration on re-ligious language was later adopted in the God-is-dead theology, especially by Paul M. van Buren. Other interpreters, with Bonhoeffer's friend and biographer Bethge as foremost au-thority, considered that to be a blunder, an inadmissible reduction of a theological program that according to them sought primarily, if not exclusively, a radical Christian ethic rather than a new philosophical hermeneutic. "Hence non-religious interpretation is more an eth-ical than a hermeneutical category and also a direct call to penitence directed at the Church and its present form — for the sake of, if one likes, the kerygma, the language" (Eberhard Bethge, *Dietrich Bonhoeffer: Man of Vision, Man of Courage*, trans. Eric Mosbacher et al., ed. Edwin Robertson [New York: Harper & Row, 1970], 783). Cf. John A. Phillips, *Christ for Us in the Theology of Dietrich Bonhoeffer* (New York: Harper & Row, 1967), 221. Cf. also Feil, *Theology of Dietrich Bonhoeffer*, 52: "hermeneutics finds reality and justification only in the context of an ethics of which it is a constituent part."

The unfortunate contrast between word and deed probably saddled the matter with a taboo for some time. An approach in line with speech-act theory that considers a word to be an action and, in line with semiotics, an action to be a "word" could in my opinion move beyond such a futile dualism (see 2.2).

This care for the divine Word Bonhoeffer inherited from his theological influences, especially Luther and Barth. The cautious way with human words, however, he learned in his parental home. When Bonhoeffer asked himself while in prison if he had changed over the past years, he could only recall that he had been converted from "phraseology to reality." The impression that his father had made on him was decisive in that respect. One remained silent rather than indulge in fashionable chatter. Words were to be weighed and carefully chosen.

The care for human words, as was practiced in his family, must have influenced his theology as well. "In the Protestant church, which is a church of the preaching of God's Word, language is no outward matter." Bonhoeffer wrote those words in a letter that will concern us later, in the spring of 1940, in response to a woman who addressed him as "Preacher" on the matter of babbling and the clichés resounding from pulpits (GS, 4:41). The criticism of much empty preaching did not, however, restrain him from continuing to advocate the proclamation of the Word. In the same letter he proposes an intensive and meditative pondering of the simple language of the Bible as a remedy for the linguistic impurity of much preaching. From the same year a fragment has been preserved with the telling title "On the Glory of the Word." In that fragment he sings the praise of the divine Word, which is not a match for the heroic glorification of the deed, at a moment that Hitler's armies were conquering Europe (GS, 4:416-17). The choice between word and deed is made in favor of the former (see 5.1).

In the years of war that followed, Bonhoeffer's faith in the power of the word seems to have been severely tested. In the letter on baptism written from prison he admits that the great words of Christian proclamation seem so difficult and so far removed that he hardly dares to speak about them. Such a statement is intriguing when one realizes that it was written by someone who in the line of Barth continued to practice theology as a theology of the Word and who only briefly before could sing the high praise of the Word. What happened to Bonhoeffer and to his opinions on speaking about God in the time in between? What disillusionment overcame him? At the same time we hear him predict in the baptismal sermon that people will "once more be called so to utter the word of God that the world will be changed and renewed by it" (LPP, 300). In this context Bonhoeffer speaks of "a new language," "liberating and redeeming." That, too, is intriguing, not in the least because those words, a half century later, express the desire of many to again speak in a liberating manner about God, however floundering and stammering amid the great silence.

Theological discourse would wrong itself should it remain deaf to Bonhoeffer's voice. The theological horizon has shifted radically in the period of half a century. But Bonhoeffer's perspective and our own are connected at a vital point: our embarrassment on speaking about God. It seems to me worthwhile to examine in this book that point of contact, as far as Bonhoeffer is concerned.

Bonhoeffer is no longer the familiar guest at the theological table that he was for a long time. If he is to take a seat, then he will at least have to be introduced. The difference in context will have to be taken into account. Speaking about God in the face of Nazism is something quite different from speaking in the face of postmodernism. The awareness of the difference in horizon can be an advantage as well as a disadvantage. The half century that separates us from Bonhoeffer can save us from short-winded actualizations, in which we would let Bonhoeffer act as ventriloquist. Just as he was not a secularist, a Latin American liberation theologian, or a conservative evangelical, so also we must not make him into a postmodern linguistic philosopher. His viewpoint is not sacred and unassailable. His impressive biography and his premature death do not alter that fact.[21] Nevertheless, I hope that this book will help prevent his theology from being prematurely retired to the mausoleum of history.

21. "Probably due to his life story and its terrible end, a halo of theological unassailability has surrounded the works of Bonhoeffer, much to their own detriment. One should destroy that halo, for Bonhoeffer's sake" (E. Jüngel, quoted by Wendel, *Studien*, 2).

2 "The Word That Changes the World"

Thoughts for a Day of Baptism

T he starting point for my reconstruction of Bonhoeffer's views on speaking about God is taken from his "Thoughts on the Day of Baptism of Dietrich Wilhelm Rüdiger Bethge," the aforementioned text written from prison. In an incisive way Bonhoeffer expresses there the impasse and the possibility of speaking about God. At the same time we encounter a crucial text in the development of his theology. The baptismal sermon is located at a crossroad. Bonhoeffer wrote the baptismal sermon in May of 1944, when he had already been incarcerated in the military prison of Tegel for a year. He thus wrote the baptismal sermon at the same time that he was peppering Bethge with his new theological insights on a "world come of age" and a "non-religious interpretation of biblical concepts" (in the letters through which he posthumously gained international fame). On April 30, 1944, in a letter containing the beginnings of his new theological explorations, he wrote, "What is bothering me incessantly is the question what Christianity really is, or indeed who Christ really is, for us today" (*LPP*, 279). In the days following Bonhoeffer must have composed his "Thoughts on the Day of Baptism" for his newly born nephew and namesake. Those thoughts served as a substitute for the baptismal sermon that he was unable to deliver because of his imprisonment.

2.1 The Crisis of Upper-Middle-Class Culture

The letter begins by placing the child to be baptized in the line of succeeding generations. By his coming the little Dietrich opens a new future, but

15

he will be able to hear about former times out of the mouth of the three or four preceding generations. His birth is for Bonhoeffer an occasion to reflect on the turning of time, challenging him to explore the contours of the future.

To begin with Bonhoeffer sketches the parental environment of little Dietrich's father, Eberhard Bethge, in a village parsonage (Bethge was the son of a church minister) where simplicity, humility, and practical vitality prevailed. He hopes greatly that the newly baptized child will share those values. Then Bonhoeffer sketches the origins of little Dietrich's mother, Renate Schleicher, daughter of Bonhoeffer's oldest sister Ursula and the lawyer, Rüdiger Schleicher, in an educated, upper-middle-class environment. It is a picture of Bonhoeffer's own parental home that he paints with a few endearing strokes. "The urban [upper-] middle-class culture . . . has led to pride in public service, intellectual achievement and leadership, and a deep-rooted sense of duty towards a great heritage and cultural tradition." Bonhoeffer hopes that the baptism child "will be thankful for its spirit and draw on the strength that it gives you" (*LPP,* 294-95).

At the same time, according to Bonhoeffer, a radical cultural shift is occurring that will entail the end of the upper-middle-class lifestyle. Both environments, that of the rural church minister and that of the old urban, upper middle class, will become a submerged world by the time the little Dietrich Bethge becomes an adult. An era will end. Bonhoeffer's words do not express the dramatic mood of a fin de siècle, however, but more the disposition of an accepting acquiescence in the inevitable. His vision is not directed nostalgically toward the past but hopefully toward the future. He is convinced that what was good in the past will survive in the new era. "The old spirit, after a time of misunderstanding and weakness, withdrawal and recovery, preservation and rehabilitation, will produce new forms" (*LPP,* 295). Bonhoeffer is quite aware of the crisis that upper-middle-class culture has reached. He even speaks in terms of revolutions (*Umwälzungen,* "upheavals") when he attempts to envision the coming years. Since January 1943 Hitler has been on the losing end, and the preparations for a putsch, in which Bonhoeffer played a role, are in full swing. He apparently expects that beyond the horizon of the approaching end of the war a social and cultural revolution will occur, the extent of which he can only surmise.

At this point he does not deal with the political system that will replace National Socialism. In prison he cannot express such thoughts openly. Will it be the democracy of western Europe or eastern Bolshevism? From the pieces that Bonhoeffer wrote in the early 1940s in the framework of his resistance activities, we know that he did not hope for either. With others among his fellow German resisters he dreamed of a third, a German possibility, between the extremes of capitalism and socialism, a form of government that would avoid the liberal individualism of the one and the anti-individualism of the other.[1]

In the baptismal sermon Bonhoeffer directs his attention to the structural and cultural changes that, in his view, will surely come about, independently of the uncertain results of the political landslides that will occur after Hitler's defeat. At a structural level he sees society becoming increasingly complex, not only through material technology (radio, automobiles, telephones) but also through bureaucratization. He speaks of "the spread of bureaucracy into almost every department of life" (*LPP*, 296) that will radically alter the face of society. He thus describes to the core the continuing process of modernization and rationalization that has taken hold of the West since modern times, but that has been accelerated in the twentieth century. Bonhoeffer points to one resulting, visible change that seems to encompass all the others: the cities will be depopulated and rural areas will become urbanized. He can only guess at what the consequences of that urbanization and industrialization will be. "Are we moving towards an age of colossal organizations and collective institutions, or will the desire of innumerable people for small, manageable, personal relationships be satisfied? Must they be mutually exclusive? Might it not be that world organizations themselves, with their wide meshes, will allow more scope for personal interests?" (*LPP*, 299). The questions remain, as does the concern for the ensuing infringement on the intimacy of the personal sphere so cherished in his own environment (see 3.4).

Who will play the leading role in the new social constellation? Bonhoeffer does not say. What type of person will become the bearer of the new culture? It seems evident to Bonhoeffer that it will no longer be the bourgeois class. He acknowledges the "actual weakness" of his environment, which was not able to cope with the new era. It is striking, however, how little

---

1. Cf. *GS*, 1:355ff. It was dependent on the course of the war how much influence the "other" Germany could exercise in the realization of its own political direction in relation to that of the Allies. The goal of the foreign trips that Bonhoeffer made under the cover of counterintelligence was to inform the Allies not only of the existence of the other Germany but also of the political independence that it pursued.

Bonhoeffer, in his description of the loss of his own culture, indulges himself in self-pity and embitterment. On the contrary, the baptismal sermon reflects a realistic attempt to assess the factual situation. There may come a "uniformity in all material and spiritual aspects of human life" (does Bonhoeffer have capitalism or socialism in mind, or both?), but also an aristocratic polity, in which a new elite, with a feeling for the quality of human values such as justice, achievement, and courage, will provide leadership. The latter is perhaps only likely if the upper-middle-class military resistance, in which Bonhoeffer participates, has a significant say in determining the future of Germany. Whatever the case, Bonhoeffer seems to be saying that it does not essentially matter for our attitude toward the future. However history is decided, "it will not be difficult for us to renounce our privileges, recognizing the justice of history. We may have to face events and changes that take no account of our wishes and our rights. But if so, we shall not give way to embittered and barren pride, but consciously submit to divine judgement, and so prove ourselves worthy to survive by identifying ourselves generously and unselfishly with the life of the community and the sufferings of our fellow human beings" (*LPP*, 299).

Even if Bonhoeffer speaks here about his social class and not about the church, the guiding thought here is provided by the theological model of *kenosis*, Christ's emptying of himself. Just as a grain of wheat that falls to the earth cannot bear fruit unless it dies (John 12:24), so will the values embodied in upper-middle-class culture only be fruitful in the future if their preservation for their own sake is surrendered.[2]

The moment of revival, however, has not yet arrived. Bonhoeffer writes, "We should not make haste. We should be able to wait." It is a time of waiting. For the interim period that separates them from the new era, during the stormy revolutions that await them, Bonhoeffer points out to the baptismal child the protection that the parental home can provide as he grows up. It will be for him "a bulwark against all dangers from within and without" (*LPP*, 295). The same parental environment that was first presented in its extroverted self-awareness, as a proud bearer of leadership, seems in a time of crisis to become a place of inwardness and reflection. "Your parents will soon be teaching you to help yourself and never to be

---

2. Cf. Frits de Lange, *Grond onder de voeten: Burgerlijkheid bij Dietrich Bonhoeffer* (Ground under the feet: Bourgeois culture in Dietrich Bonhoeffer) (Kampen: Kok, 1985), 313.

afraid of soiling your hands. The piety of your home will not be noisy or loquacious, but it will teach you to say your prayers, to fear and love God above everything, and to do the will of Jesus Christ" (*LPP*, 296).

The awareness of the "submerged world" that upper-middle-class culture will become does not decrease for Bonhoeffer the importance of upper-middle-class values as such. His faith in values such as simplicity, a concentrated and varied intellectual life, appreciation of the small things in life, humility, but also intellectual achievement, leadership, and care for tradition is apparently unshaken. He speaks of "enduring values." That the way in which they take form is radically changing does not deter from the fact that they are still to be cherished. The "old spirit" will have to find "new forms," but which ones, how and when, remains to be seen.

2.2 Reconciling and Redeeming, Shocking and Overwhelming (The Performative Power of the Word)

That last statement is important for Bonhoeffer's view of the future of Christian faith. In the following fragment of the baptismal sermon we find intriguing sentences on "earlier words" that will "lose their force" and the expectation of a "new language" that will be "liberating and redeeming."

> Today you will be baptized a Christian. All those great ancient words of the Christian proclamation will be spoken over you, and the command of Jesus Christ to baptize will be carried out on you, without your knowing anything about it. But we are once again being driven right back to the beginnings of our understanding. Reconciliation and redemption, regeneration and the Holy Spirit, love of our enemies, cross and resurrection, life in Christ and Christian discipleship — all these things are so difficult and so remote that we hardly venture any more to speak of them. In the traditional words and acts we suspect that there may be something quite new and revolutionary, though we cannot as yet grasp or express it. That is our own fault. Our church, which has been fighting in these years only for its self-preservation, as though that were an end in itself, is incapable of taking the word of reconciliation and redemption to mankind and the world. Our earlier words are therefore bound to lose their force and cease, and our being Christians today will be limited to two things: prayer and righteous action among men. All Christian thinking, speaking, and organizing must be born anew out of this

prayer and action. By the time you have grown up, the church's form will have changed greatly. We are not yet out of the melting-pot, and any attempt to help the church prematurely to a new expansion of its organization will merely delay its conversion and purification. It is not for us to prophesy the day (though the day will come) when men will once more be called so to utter the word of God that the world will be changed and renewed by it. It will be a new language, perhaps quite non-religious, but liberating and redeeming — as was Jesus' language; it will shock people and yet overcome them by its power; it will be the language of a new righteousness and truth, proclaiming God's peace with men and the coming of his kingdom. "They shall fear and tremble because of all the good and all the prosperity I provide for it" (Jer. 33.9). Till then the Christian cause will be a silent and hidden affair, but there will be those who pray and act to achieve justice and wait for God's own time. May you be one of them, and may it be said of you one day, "The path of the righteous is like the light of dawn, which shines brighter and brighter till full day" (Prov. 4.18). (*LPP*, 299-300)

The conclusion of the "Thoughts on the Day of Baptism" parallels the opening paragraph. The future of the church seems to bear a structural similarity to that of upper-middle-class culture, as sketched above. Bonhoeffer does not in this respect advocate breaking with tradition, but sees a metamorphosis taking place, to which the only adequate response is that of active waiting.

While Bonhoeffer had to acknowledge the powerlessness of upper-middle-class culture within the new constellation, nevertheless, he saw a future role for the "old spirit" that inspired those "enduring earthly values." Likewise he saw a hopeful perspective for the "grand old words of Christian proclamation" that would be spoken over the child by the administration of the sacrament. The words *reconciliation, redemption, rebirth,* and so on had not been played out for Bonhoeffer. On the contrary, he suspected that there is an unknown, hidden potential of revolutionary power in those words. The words *reconciliation, redemption, rebirth,* and so on seem to Bonhoeffer to be full of vitality. "In the traditional words and acts we suspect that there may be something quite new and revolutionary, though we cannot as yet grasp or express it" (*LPP*, 300). He seems to have an as yet outstanding surplus of meaning in mind, rather than a deficit of meaning. His faith in a God who speaks about God seems unbroken. The crisis of speaking in the church is apparently not to be derived from the silence of God. It is not due to God that God can only scarcely and with difficulty be spoken of. Bonhoeffer expresses the expectation, and he is even certain, that the day will come when the new and revolutionary power that is smoldering and glowing in the Word of God will burst into flame. The day will come that people will again be called to speak the same Word of God in such a way that "the word will be changed and renewed by it" (*LPP*, 300). The word is like a grain of wheat in a field that yields a large harvest.

With almost explosive language Bonhoeffer speaks of the power of the God-given word. It is a word that "reconciles and redeems," a language that shocks and overcomes, with such power that it overwhelms by its authority. The evocative and effective Word of God taps a dimension of language that has a salutary effect on the listeners.

What sort of language does God speak? With a clarifying distinction from modern language theory, one can say that the Word of God is not constative but performative language.

A *constative* speech act refers to a state of affairs that already exists in reality. The enactment in such a use of language is that of determination. A constative statement indicates *what is*. A *performative* speech act, on the other hand, creates the reality to which it refers in the act of speaking. It possesses the power to create a reality that did not yet exist.

The distinction between constative and performative speech acts originates from the English linguistic philosopher J. L. Austin. It was refined and advanced in the so-called speech-act theory, particularly by John R. Searle. In that theory language is considered to be a form of behavior and speech to be an act. In keeping with Wittgenstein, speech is viewed as an act that takes on meaning within a specific social context in which it is interpreted. When people say something, they do something, and the meaning of their speech lies in the usage they make of language.

Austin's "discovery" can be traced back to the insight that no fundamental distinction exists between a word and an act or deed. With words one also enacts a deed. Language is not only able to describe reality *(mimesis)*, but also to shape and change reality *(poiesis)*. Austin placed great emphasis on this, in his view, neglected dimension of language. What do people do when they say something? They assert, promise, declare, ask, command, order, request, invite, warn, observe, greet, demand, argue, obey, testify, and so on. Austin calls the act that is effected in making an utterance a *performative* act.

One also does something when one describes a state of affairs. Every utterance, even a constative one, has in that sense a performative aspect. Austin, however, was primarily interested in those acts of speech with an *explicit* performative character. The preeminent example in this respect is the making of a promise. A promise creates a relation of mutual obligation and expectation that did not exist before. (For example: "I promise that I will return your book tomorrow.") A queen who names a ship or a church minister who baptizes a child employs performative speech. The utterance "I name you the *Queen Elizabeth*," or "I baptize you in the name of the Father, the Son, and the Holy Spirit," is to be understood as the "performance of an act *in* saying something."[3]

Bonhoeffer was not primarily concerned with shortcomings in the constative capacities of religious language, but with its lacking ability to create and transform reality. The "new language" for which Bonhoeffer hoped does not so much distinguish itself from the old language by being able to describe what the older cannot (i.e., can no longer or cannot yet describe),[4] but by the fact that it, contrary to the old language, is "liberating and redeeming." Whether the new language is religious or "perhaps" (as Bonhoeffer cautiously adds) nonreligious is not essential. Whether the preaching has a saving effect is decisive. And nonreligious language is to be preferred if it is more helpful in that respect than religious language. (It seems clear that Bonhoeffer thinks so. See 6.1.)

From what source is the new language to derive its powerful, performative effect? In a brief addition Bonhoeffer indicates clearly the direction for Christian proclamation. It will be liberating and redeeming

3. J. L. Austin, *How to Do Things with Words,* 2d ed. (Oxford: Oxford University Press, 1975), 99-100. Cf. John R. Searle, *Speech Acts: An Essay in the Philosophy of Language* (London: Cambridge University Press, 1969), 22-23. For a theological reception of these theories of language-acts see, e.g., R. Wonneberger and H. P. Hecht, *Verheißung und Versprechen: Eine theologische und sprachanalytische Klärung* (Promise and vow: A theological and linguistic analysis) (Göttingen: Vandenhoeck & Ruprecht, 1986); and H. Weder, *Neutestamentische Hermeneutik* (New Testament hermeneutics) (Zurich: Theologischer Verlag, 1986), esp. 166ff. For application in homiletics, cf. D. Zilleßen, ed., *Praktisch-theologische Hermeneutik* (Practical-theological hermeneutics) (Rheimbach-Merzbach: CMZ-Verlag, 1991), 181-207 and 371-83.

4. J. Sperna Weiland, *Het einde van de religie: Verder op het spoor van Bonhoeffer* (The end of religion: Pursuing the path of Bonhoeffer) (Baarn: Het Wereldvenster, 1970), 85, seems to think in that direction. He considers the last outline of Bonhoeffer to be a farewell to the language of metaphysics. *Letters and Papers from Prison* is "a wrestling with the language in which things have to be said that are hidden from view by language, as is the case in the later writings of Heidegger. With both there is an attempt to write in language beyond language" (see 100 and 188).

"like the language of Jesus." Jesus' speaking provoked astonishment and awe, and people yielded themselves to its power. Jesus spoke a language of a "new justice" (is this Paul speaking?), of "truth" (John?), "a language proclaiming God's peace with people and the coming of God's kingdom" (the Synoptics?). With a great biblical pluriformity, the gospel speaks an "effectuating" language that addresses people in order to transform them. That occurs by means of a concrete confrontation with the person of Jesus and the appeal that issues from him.

Here Bonhoeffer touches on the heart of Jesus' proclamation of the kingdom of God and of Pauline description of the gospel as a saving, transforming power of God in the history of humankind.

The word *euangelion* goes back to the Old Testament Hebrew verb *bśr*, which indicates the proclamation of a (good, joyful) message (1 Kgs. 1:42; Jer. 20:15; 2 Sam. 4:10; 18:26). In Deutero-Isaiah it is used within the framework of the proclamation of the universal sovereignty of God (Isa. 52:7-10; cf. 40:9; 41:27; 61:1; also Nah. 2:1). The picture is that of (1) an eschatological expectation ("the messenger, *mebaśśer*, who announces peace"), with (2) a universal character (the gentiles, "all the nations," are included), (3) whose content is the sovereignty of God ("Your God is king"), and (4) that brings joy and peace. The proclamation of the reign of God is at the same time its beginning. Salvation is enacted in its proclamation. The act of proclamation and its content are fused: the latter is effectuated in the former. The God who is spoken of as king *is* king at that moment. The announcement of the coming of the kingdom is a form of performative speaking.

In the New Testament the elements pointed to in Deutero-Isaiah are again present, centered around the person of Jesus (see Rom. 10:15). He is the bearer of eschatological salvation (Matt. 11:5; Luke 7:22), the eschatological evangelist (Mark 1:14-15), who in his proclamation and actions represents the salvation of God and who possesses the competence to do so by means of his God-given *exousia* (authority, empowerment).

Conversion and belief in the kingdom of God are named by Jesus in one breath. The reverse side of the proclaimed salvation is the judgment on and conversion in the life of the hearer. The indicative of the kingdom of God implies the imperative of the *metanoia* or "change of attitude."[5]

5. J. Behm, *Theological Dictionary of the New Testament*, ed. G. Kittel and G. Friedrich, trans. and ed. G. W. Bromiley, 10 vols. (Grand Rapids: Eerdmans, 1964-76), 4:1001.

Faith *(pistis)* is the fruit of conversion, but the reverse is also true (Mark 1:15). The hard and unconditional character of the call to transformation of one's existence is one with the healing offer of grace (cf. Matt. 11:28ff.). *Metanoia* and *soteria,* conversion and salvation, belong together. One cannot hear the gospel without being spoken to, moved, touched, and changed by it. Conversion is a condition and a direct result of understanding the message of salvation. Jesus can even describe the entire purpose of his mission in terms of conversion. "I have come to call not the righteous but sinners to repentance" (Luke 5:32; cf. Matt. 11:20). The experience of the nearness of the kingdom of God implies a total transformation that affects the very center of a person's existence. It leads to a turning away from evil and a turning toward God.

After Easter Jesus, the unique "exegete of God" (John 1:18), becomes as bearer of salvation its content as well. The Proclaimer becomes the Proclaimed. But for Paul as well *euangelio* indicates both the act of proclamation and the content of proclamation, even if the latter has become identical with the story of Jesus' suffering, death, and resurrection (cf. 1 Cor. 9:14, 18). The *euangelion* enacts itself, just as with Jesus, in the proclamation. It is a performative act. Paul's doctrine of righteousness is in this respect on a line with Jesus' healing and forgiving word of salvation. Both break into the life situation of people and change it. "Our message of the gospel did not come to you in word only, but in power and in fullness" (1 Thess. 1:5-6). Proclamation itself is an eschatological event. One undergoes the workings of a "power for salvation" *(dynamis eis soterion,* Rom. 1:16). The apostle himself has undergone the transforming dynamic. The gospel astonished him and forced him to his knees (Damascus!).[6]

2.3 "It Is Our Own Fault"
   (The Pragmatic Context)

How could Jesus, and like him the apostles, do what we cannot, or at least no longer can? What is to blame for the present inability to speak a liberating language? It is not a lack of creative or narrative capacity of language. Nor is it a lack of verbal creativity and fantasy among theologians. What is it then?

6. On this fundamental performative character of New Testament speech see Weder, *Neutestamentische Hermeneutik,* 173ff.; "Faith belongs to the Word of God just as laughter belongs to the joke" (236).

Bonhoeffer allows no room for misunderstanding and answers with a terse statement. "That is our own fault. Our church, which has been fighting in these years only for its self-preservation, as though that were an end in itself, is incapable of taking the word of reconciliation and redemption to mankind and the world" (*LPP,* 299). It is the proclaiming church itself that makes its proclamation incredible. Apparently it lacks the *exousia* that the words of Jesus possessed. The act of proclaiming the gospel is still performed from the pulpits, but the language fails. It has no effect.

The speaker lacks competence. Consequently, we can no longer appreciate the meaning of the old words of Christian tradition. But, to put it in terms of a distinction from linguistic science, the pain that we feel in Christian semantics (which pertains to the meaning of faith language) is a symptom of an ailment that is located primarily in Christian pragmatics (the relation between the speaker and what is spoken). The church no longer measures up to its proclamation. For that reason its word returns empty (see Isa. 55:11).

Again an excursion to the theory of "speech-acts" can help to clarify things. The theory emphasizes that the act of speaking is embedded in a social context, of which the speaker and the hearer are both a part. In keeping with the later Wittgenstein, language is seen as a pluriform complex of language games. (Commanding, describing, telling stories, greeting, requesting, but also praying, thanking, and cursing are examples that Wittgenstein himself mentions.) The rules of the language games are expressions of "shared practices" and represent specific social "life forms."[7] Language, including religious language, is apparently deeply rooted in conventions, institutionalized forms of human behavior.

The "performance" of a language act can only succeed under certain conditions. At the least specific communicative and institutional conditions must be met for them to be effective. For some language acts it is enough when the rules of language itself are satisfied. An example is promises, introduced by "I promise you . . ." or by use of the future tense ("I shall . . ."). Promises are not usually confined to one specific social setting. One can make them anywhere. For other language acts specific institutional conditions have to be satisfied.[8] The statement "I baptize you in the name of the Father, the Son, and the Holy Spirit," is effective only in the church, not as child's play in a bath. In the latter case the conditional

---

7. Wittgenstein, *Philosophical Investigations,* §23.

8. J. R. Searle, *Expression and Meaning: Studies in the Theory of Speech Acts* (Cambridge: Cambridge University Press, 1979), 17-18.

cultural framework is lacking. In all cases, however, words become operational, have "authority," only if they obtain authority, *exousia*, from those involved in a specific context. In the case of the judge who acquits, the policeman who fines, the queen who opens parliament, the priest or preacher who administers the sacraments or utters the benediction, their acquittal, fine, and so on are enacted only when the one speaking is competent to do so. They do not possess the competence by nature, for it must be granted to them by the social surroundings within which they speak. (They have to "earn" it.) If what they say is to be effective, then those being addressed must *attribute* to those speaking the authority that is claimed by so speaking. The salutary effect of Jesus' words — "Your sins are forgiven you" or "Blessed are the poor in spirit" — can be experienced only if the hearer considers Jesus competent in matters of the forgiveness of sins and blessing. That implies a creative and productive function on the part of those addressed. They contribute to the acquisition of meaning of what they hear. A condition for the success of a language act is a relation in which the speaker and those spoken to confirm each other in their positions, in a *mutual recognition of who they are for each other.*

In Bonhoeffer's view the church's speaking on God has become powerless, because the church has forfeited its competence to speak. What is the cause of that? Bonhoeffer points to a church that has fought only for its self-preservation, as if it were an end in itself. That posture is the cause of its incapacity to speak in a liberating fashion about God, to take "the word of reconciliation and redemption to humankind and the world. Our earlier words are *therefore* bound to lose their force and cease."[9]

The failure of Christian proclamation is not located by Bonhoeffer in the content of proclamation as such, but rather in the *pragmatic context* in which the church speaks. A pragmatic context can be divided into three elements, depending on whether one provides a broader or narrower description of it. There is (1) the *person* speaking (and the person spoken to), (2) the *institutional framework*, the mutually recognized pattern of social actions (conventions) within which both encounter each other, and finally, (3) the historical and cultural *situation* in which it occurs.[10] In all, three

9. *LPP,* 299, emphasis mine.

10. K. F. Daiber, *Predigen und Hören,* vol. 2: *Kommunikation zwischen Predigern und Hörern — Sozialwissenschaftliche Untersuchungen* (Preaching and hearing, vol. 2: Communication between preachers and hearers — a social-scientific investigation) (Munich: Chr. Kaiser, 1983), 71, 86. The personal context is described as micropragmatic and the situational context as macropragmatic.

specific conditions have to be created if successful communication (understood as transfer of meanings) is to occur.

Those three elements can be found in Bonhoeffer's writings. First, a person has to be accountable for the truth of what is said and for the desired effect in the hearer. Applied to the proclamation of the gospel, that means that Christians, who testify to others of their faith, are answerable for the life-changing truth of the testimony source as they want to share the liberation and salvation it provides. In that respect Bonhoeffer points in his prison letters to a poignant lack of *personal faith* (*ad* 1). In the "Outline for a Book" he does not spare believers his criticism, even if they be members of the Confessing Church who gave evidence of courage simply by means of their membership. "Generally in the Confessing Church: standing up for the church's 'cause,' etc., but little personal faith in Christ. 'Jesus' is disappearing from sight" (*LPP*, 381). We know from *The Cost of Discipleship* how much Bonhoeffer adhered to a direct orientation in life to the person of Jesus. He identified faith in Jesus with obedience to Jesus' word. In the letters we notice that he still advocates such a Jesus-centered radicalness. In the "Outline for a Book" we read that Bonhoeffer does not want to measure the faith of a Christian by the amount of doctrine to which one subscribes. Bonhoeffer makes the question "What do we really believe?" more specific by adding, "I mean, believe in such a way, that we stake our lives on it?" (*LPP*, 382). Faith for Bonhoeffer is a capital affair that demands our total commitment to the cause of Jesus.

In a letter to Bethge on the occasion of Easter 1944, written from his prison cell on March 27 of that year, Bonhoeffer speaks of the death and resurrection of Christ. From the event of Easter "a new and purifying wind can blow through our present world. . . . If a few people really believed it and acted on it in their daily lives, a great deal would be changed. To live in the light of the resurrection — that is what Easter means." It becomes clear the extent to which Bonhoeffer measures the Christian word by its transforming power and the extent to which he considers it to be dependent on personal credibility. He proceeds in the letter with a question for Bethge, whether he would agree that most people do not know by what they live. In that context we hear Bonhoeffer speaking of the importance of personal commitment for Christians. The words are almost literally identical with the words of the letter on baptism, a month later. "This *perturbatio animorum* [confusion of the spirits] spreads amazingly. It's an unconscious waiting for the word of deliverance, though the time is probably not yet ripe for it to be heard. But the time will come, and this Easter may be one of our last chances to prepare ourselves for our great task of the future" (*LPP*, 240-41).[11]

The church lives by the story of Jesus, who gave his life for others. That is its ground of existence. Decisive for the Confessing Church, however, is Bonhoeffer's observation: "The church on the defensive. No taking risks for others" (*LPP*, 381). Here we confront a second element that affects the pragmatic context of speaking about God (*ad* 2), the institutional framework of the church. If words are to have effect, they must be supported, and at any rate not contradicted, by the practices in which they function. They derive their legitimation and validity not only from personal credibility but also from their institutional context. The statement, "I guarantee it's a good car!" sounds different coming from a certified automobile dealer than on a second-hand car lot, even if it be sincerely meant in both cases. The request, "Lend me a hundred dollars. I'll pay you back tomorrow," has more chance of succeeding when spoken to a colleague than when spoken in a casino. It is possible that the first word spoken from a pulpit will lack validity, simply because it is being spoken from a pulpit. ("So much has already been said, and in the meantime. . . .") Here again it is clear for Bonhoeffer that the proclamation of the gospel runs up against an insurmountable obstacle. The fixation of the church on its self-preservation runs contrary to the ethics of the Christ it proclaims, as a person who risked his life for others.

Herein lies a significant cause of the disappointment of Bonhoeffer in the direction "his" Confessing Church took. It stood up only for itself. With great difficulty and display of courage it established its own space in a totalitarian state. But it did not put its commitment to the service of others whose humanity was being violated outside the walls of the church. It stood up for itself but did not, as Bonhoeffer did by his participation in political resistance, stand up for Germany in general and for the Jews in particular. Since the introduction of the "Aryan Clause" in 1933 (which denied Jews public office, including that of functioning as

---

11. Bonhoeffer probably refers here to the anticipated assassination of Hitler, the planned coup d'état, and the resulting new relations between church and world. Cf. *LPP*, 278: "I have such a feeling that great events are moving the world every day and could change all our personal relationships" (April 30, 1944), and *LPP*, 290: "My own opinion is that the next few weeks will bring such great and surprising events" (May 9, 1944).

church minister), Bonhoeffer had tirelessly applied himself to the cause of the Jews.[12]

Two words of Bonhoeffer, both of which refer explicitly to the church's speaking on God, are significant in this context. The first is a verse of the biblical book of Proverbs, a verse that Bonhoeffer incessantly quoted in the 1930s: "Speak out for those who cannot speak" (Prov. 31:8).[13] For Bonhoeffer the element of substitution, proxy, in the doctrine of reconciliation was no dormant matter but constituted the heart of Christian ethics and of ecclesiology. The church is to be for others just as Jesus was. The Jews were denied fundamental human rights. They had no means of defense against their own government. Bonhoeffer expected the church to take up the cause of the silenced Jews and speak up for them. In a confession of guilt from the year 1940 Bonhoeffer wrote this of the church: "It was silent when it should have cried out because the blood of the innocent was crying aloud to heaven. It has failed to speak the right word in the right way and at the right time" (E, 92).

"Only he who shouts for the Jews can sing the Gregorian chant." This second word of Bonhoeffer is important in this context.[14] Bonhoeffer resisted the political hesitations that the Lutheran tradition of two kingdoms had engendered in his church. Besides a call to political involvement, the statement also includes a polemic against certain renewal movements in the German church (such as the Oxford and Berneuchner movements) that pursued a new vitality for the church by means of liturgical reform.[15]

12. For a detailed description and analysis of Bonhoeffer's position on the Jewish question in relation to that of the Protestant church and in circles of German resistance, see C.-R. Müller, *Dietrich Bonhoeffers Kampf gegen die nationalsozialistische Verfolgung und Vernichtung der Juden* (Dietrich Bonhoeffer's struggle against the National Socialist persecution and extermination of the Jews) (Munich: Chr. Kaiser, 1990).

13. Bethge, *Dietrich Bonhoeffer*, 207, 334, 407, 435, 445. Cf. *TF*, 412: "We must also finally do away with the theologically grounded restrictions in regard to action by the state — after all, it is only fear. 'Speak out for those who cannot speak' (Prov. 31:8). Who still knows that in the church today, this is the least requirement of the Bible in such times?" (letter to E. Sütz, September 11, 1934); cf. also *GS*, 2:144, 415; also 323-24; *CD*, 289.

14. Bethge, *Dietrich Bonhoeffer*, 360-61.

15. Bonhoeffer was again confronted with the Berneuchen movement when in 1942 he met his later fiancée, Maria von Wedemeyer. Her father, Max von Wedemeyer, was an advocate of the movement. See *LL*, 306-8. For a further description of the relation between the Berneuchner movement and the Confessing Church see R. Mayer, "Braut-

In the letter on baptism, however, Bonhoeffer does not choose an easy goal for his criticism. The German Evangelical (Protestant) Church had accommodated itself totally to becoming a mouthpiece and an extension of the Nazi regime. Bonhoeffer's criticism was directed primarily at his own Confessing Church, which had courageously resisted such accommodation but had not employed its courage for the sake of the Jews.[16]

2.4 A Religionless Era

Besides criticism of the lack of moral action and faithful commitment to the cause of Jesus in the Confessing Church, Bonhoeffer also criticizes the church's failure to confront the new cultural *situation* (*ad* 3) in which its proclamation resounds. Here we come upon the third element of the pragmatic context of speaking about God that Bonhoeffer considers responsible for the powerlessness of the proclamation. He points to a "changing of the times" and expects "coming years of revolution," as we read at the beginning of his baptismal sermon. At the end of it we hear that the church is also involved in a "smelting process." Its form will change radically in Bonhoeffer's expectation. But are the church and theology prepared for that?

The "situation" in this context includes everything that determines the horizon of the culture in a specific era. It is a macroterm that describes the values, norms, and understandings by which people orient themselves and with which they provide their lives with direction and meaning. That situation, however vague and undetermined it may be, should be subjected to a cultural analysis. According to Bonhoeffer, theology cannot ignore the necessity of such an analysis. If the communication between church and

---

briefe aus der Zelle" (Love letter from the cell), in R. Mayer and P. Zimmerling, *Dietrich Bonhoeffer — Mensch hinter Mauern: Theologie und Spiritualität in den Gefängnisjahren* (Dietrich Bonhoeffer — man behind walls: Theology and spirituality during the years of imprisonment) (Giessen/Basel: Brunnen, 1993), 69-98, esp. 76ff.

16. Bethge, *Dietrich Bonhoeffer*, 593: "When the 'final solution' of the Jewish question was begun in the autumn of 1941, what was left of the Confessing Church was fully occupied with questions concerning its own existence, and there were only a few brave isolated actions." Bethge points out how Bonhoeffer "made this question into a criterion for every declaration of his Confessing Church" (Bethge, *Am gegebenen Ort: Aufsätze und Reden, 1970-1979* [At the given place: Essays and speeches, 1970-1979] [Munich: Chr. Kaiser, 1979], 232).

world is not to fail and if the word of the gospel is to be effective, then culture and church will need to confirm each other in their relative positions, "in a mutual recognition of who we are for each other," as has been formulated above (2.3). Both must know who is speaking and who is being addressed.

The proclamation of the gospel has an address. Bonhoeffer's theological explorations in prison were directed not only at the credibility of the sender (the Christian person and the church as institution) but also at becoming familiar with the addressee (in his terms: the religionless person in a world come of age). In the letter of April 30, 1944, in which Bonhoeffer launches his radical theological explorations, we read: "What is bothering me incessantly is the question what Christianity really is, or indeed who Christ really is, for us today. The time when people could be told everything by means of words, whether theological or pious, is over, and so is the time of inwardness and conscience — and that means the time of religion in general. We are moving toward a completely religionless time; people as they are now simply cannot be religious any more" (*LPP*, 279).

Here also Bonhoeffer points explicitly to the shortcomings of verbal proclamation. But now his sight is not so much directed at the situation of the speaker who does not live up to his or her word, nor at the church that by its fixation on its own self-preservation makes its proclamation incredible, but at the addressee, the person who is to be touched and transformed by the Word of God. Why does the Word not get across? We encounter here a third cause. The era of the domination of speaking as such is past. The spoken and written word no longer has a monopoly in the communication of meaning.

It is not clear precisely which cultural shifts Bonhoeffer had in mind. Even with the help of the other letters it does not become clear and distinct. Perhaps he himself had only vague suspicions. What seems certain is that in the cultural shift that Bonhoeffer expected, the role of conscience, of inwardness, and of the word as a medium of religious communication would decline. Bonhoeffer knew all too well as we saw in the baptismal sermon that modernization entails technicization and that technology radically alters the cultural landscape. He acknowledged that the end of the upper-middle-class way of life was near. But he could not have suspected that not only "radio, car, and telephone" but also the screen would dominate modern experience. Would he be able to subscribe to the typology of David Riesman, who shortly after the war, in *The Lonely Crowd*, contrasted the middle-class and post-middle-class types as being "inner-directed" and "outer-directed," respectively? Whereas the former is guided by the inner compass of his or her personal conscience, the latter sets course by keeping an eye on the radar of his or her social environment.[17] The "speaking human" will lose out to the "seeing human." What does that mean for preaching in the church? Bonhoeffer did not develop his thoughts on such matters, and we should not try to put any such ideas in his mouth.

Nevertheless, in Bonhoeffer's view, the cultural land shifts have to be recognized. At the same time he considered the church incapable of such insight. The church maintained not only a theology that was lacking but also an outdated sociology. In his "Outline for a Book" we read that the church has made the gospel incredible by its lack of personal faith and by its concern for self-preservation. But also that it fails to connect with the life experience of modern people: "The Protestant church: Pietism as a last attempt to maintain evangelical Christianity as a religion; Lutheran orthodoxy, the attempt to rescue the church as an institution for salvation; the Confessing Church: the theology of revelation; a *dos moi pou stoi*[18] over against the world. . . . Sociologically: no effect on the masses — interest confined to the upper and lower middle classes. A heavy incubus of difficult traditional ideas" (*LPP*, 381).

Similar words can be found in Bonhoeffer's letter of June 8, 1944. There he develops his thoughts on a world come of age and the nonreligious interpretation of theological concepts that seems to him to be called for in that context. He then notes that the focus on revelation, in which the Confessing Church initially pursued the line of Barth, has in the meantime turned into what he calls "conservative restoration." It "is of significance because it holds onto the great concepts of Christian theology, but that seems to be about all that can be said of it." The tradition, according to Bonhoeffer's criticism, remains "undeveloped" and "remote," the latter word being one that we encountered in the baptismal sermon. "There is no interpretation" (*LPP*, 328). That means, we may conclude, that Christian tradition is not translated into terms of the self-understanding of a world

17. David Riesman, *The Lonely Crowd: A Study of the Changing American Character* (New Haven: Yale University Press, 1950).

18. "Give me somewhere to stand, and I will move the earth," a quotation from Archimedes. Cf. *LPP*, 240.

come of age and a religionless humankind, such as is characteristic of the cultural situation that is part of the pragmatic context for the church's speaking about God.

How did Bonhoeffer envision the progression of the culture that he sees lying beyond the collapse of the Third Reich? The contours remain vague, but with a few lines he did sketch its horizons. In the baptismal sermon Bonhoeffer described the more *structural* dimensions of the process of modernization, the "spread of bureaucracy into almost every department of life," that accompanied society becoming more complex. In the "Outline for a Book," and even more in the letters that he wrote to Eberhard Bethge from April 30, 1944, on, he dealt with that again and tried to discern the cultural consequences of that process with regard to their significance for speaking about God. In the letter of June 8, 1944, he wants to say "a little more about the historical situation." He notes that not only the church but also theologians (he mentions Karl Heim, Paul Althaus, Paul Tillich, and Karl Barth) have responded inadequately (*LPP*, 327-28). "The question is: Christ and the world that has come of age." Bonhoeffer's conclusion from the work of Barth is that "in the non-religious interpretation of theological concepts he gave no concrete guidance, either in dogmatics or in ethics" (*LPP*, 328).

The intention of Bonhoeffer's theological program in this context is described in a single, terse sentence somewhat further in the same letter. "The world's coming of age is no longer an occasion for polemics and apologetics, but is now really better understood than it understands itself, namely on the basis of the gospel and in the light of Christ" (*LPP*, 329). Whether that program succeeded in its intention is debatable. In the last chapter I return to his outline. Here my only concern is to note what drove him to his search: the realization that the church in its speaking about God was not aware of the altered historical and cultural situation, encompassing both the speaker and the one spoken to.

2.5 A New Language

What does all this mean for the content of the proclamation of the church? Perhaps it was not all clear even to Bonhoeffer. In the letter of May 5, 1944, we can read: "I am thinking about how we can reinterpret in a 'worldly' sense — in the sense of the Old Testament and of John 1.14 — the concepts of repentance, faith, justification, rebirth, and sanctification" (*LPP*, 286-87). In the "Thoughts on the Day of Baptism," he asks the same with regard to reconciliation and redemption, regeneration and the Holy Spirit, love of our enemies, cross and resurrection, life in Christ and Christian discipleship (*LPP*, 299). But in the "Outline for a Book" he does not get beyond a sort of listing of wishes: "Interpretation of biblical concepts on this basis. (Creation, fall, atonement, repentance, faith, the new life, the last things.)" (*LPP*, 382). Possibly Bonhoeffer envisioned a hermeneutical "program of translation." It is clear in any case that he was unable to carry it out.[19]

It is to be doubted whether Bonhoeffer, with the "new language" for which he hoped, only had in mind a theological hermeneutic (in the sense of an interpretive method for reading the old, no longer familiar texts). We already saw that he located the Christian impotence not primarily in the semantic dimension of proclamation (what is the meaning of the gospel?), but in the pragmatic sphere (how can the gospel again become liberating and renewing?). In that respect the altered cultural situation constitutes an important component, but alongside two other aspects (personal commitment and credible church structures).

In addition Bonhoeffer seemed to emphasize the importance of insight into the limits of words. "Our being Christians today will be limited to two things: prayer and righteous action among men," according to the baptismal sermon (*LPP*, 300). As long as the new language, liberating and redeeming like the language of Jesus, does not resound, then the gospel will apparently be communicated by people who speak a sort of interim language, people who "pray and do right and wait for God's own time." If Bonhoeffer was hoping for a new theological hermeneutic, then in any case it was one that sought to understand a different language than just the spoken and written word.

Bonhoeffer seemed to expect a time in which the public significance

19. Others have tried this since him. Cf., e.g., Paul M. van Buren, *The Secular Meaning of the Gospel, Based on an Analysis of Its Language* (New York: Macmillan, 1963). A couple of Dutch attempts, both emphatically "in the line of Bonhoeffer," are J. Sperna Weiland, *Het einde van de religie: Verder op het spoor van Bonhoeffer* (The end of religion: Pursuing the path of Bonhoeffer) (see n. 4 above); and Herman Wiersinga, *Geloven bij daglicht: Verlies en toekomst van een traditie* (Believing by daylight: Loss and future of a tradition) (Baarn: Ten Have, 1992).

of church proclamation would severely decline. The parallel with the previously described fate of upper-middle-class culture is striking. The piety of the parental home "will not be noisy or loquacious," but marked by prayer, the fear and love of God, and doing the will of Jesus, as we saw above (*LPP*, 296). The same holds for the interim form of the church. The period of moratorium until a new, liberating manner of speaking about God arises will be a time of conversion and purification. "All Christian thinking, speaking, and organizing must be born anew out of this prayer and action" (*LPP*, 300). The cause of Christians will until then be "silent and hidden." Any attempt to run ahead hurriedly will, in Bonhoeffer's opinion, turn itself against the church.

How long that time will last we do not know. The church, however, will have to adjust to a situation in which the spoken and written word assume a more modest tone. "The time of a pious or theological word is past." That is so for two reasons, as we now know. The potentialities of the word are limited by the cultural *situation,* but not by that alone. The word of the church has above all been shattered by the church's actions. The proclamation of the word has become incredible due to a lack of *personal faith* and to the *shape of a church* focused on self-preservation. Prayer and doing justice seem for the time being to be the only language that can communicate the meaning of the gospel unambiguously.

Does that detract from the richness of the Word of God? I suspect that Bonhoeffer thought the opposite. In this situation the church, to be sure, will be thrust back onto its religious essence. We will yet see how in his opinion Christian speaking about God arises out of a respectful silence before God's presence (5.4). The heart of the life of faith lies enfolded in the silence of *prayer.* There, at the spring from which any speaking about God is to refresh itself, we encounter the limits of the word.[20] "In the end, silence means nothing other than waiting for God's Word and coming from God's Word with a blessing." So we read in *Life Together,* the fruit of his spiritual experiment in Finkenwalde from 1938 (*LT,* 85). It is the same waiting attitude that Bonhoeffer advocates in the baptismal sermon for the

20. On the essential significance of prayer for the theology of Bonhoeffer, cf. A. Altenähr, *Dietrich Bonhoeffer als Lehrer des Gebetes* (Dietrich Bonhoeffer as teacher of prayer) (Würzburg: Echter, 1976); E. Bethge, *Zwischen Finkenwalde und Tirpitzufer: Der Ort des Gebetes in Leben und Theologie von Dietrich Bonhoeffer* (Between Finkenwalde and Tirpitzufer: The place of prayer in the life and theology of Dietrich Bonhoeffer) (Kampen: Kok, 1984).

church as a whole. It is a silence that comes forth out of a surplus, not a deficit, of the Word.

In this context Bonhoeffer makes his proposal for a renewal of the *disciplina arcani* of the early church. "There are degrees of knowledge and degrees of significance; that means that a secret discipline must be restored whereby the *mysteries* of the Christian faith are protected against profanation." Thus Bonhoeffer writes in response to what he considers to be Barth's positivist doctrine of revelation, in which each part of the teaching of faith is taken to be of equal weight (*LPP*, 286). We shall need to return to what Bonhoeffer is getting at here. His utterances remain vague. But I offer at this point the suggestion that "profanation" at the least means trying to put everything into words. The arcanum, the mystery of faith, transcends the limits of language.

That is true as well for doing justice, of which Bonhoeffer speaks in the baptismal sermon. The church's actions must surpass the ambivalence of "saying one thing and doing another." What Bonhoeffer has in mind we can read in the last chapter of the book that he wanted to write in prison. In the outline that has been preserved (for the book has been lost), he indicates the shape of a church that has moved beyond its incapacity. The passage begins with the sentence, "The church is the church only when it exists for others," and continues with an enumeration of what that entails in practice. The property of the church must be given to the needy. The clergy will have to "live solely on the free-will offerings of their congregations, or possibly engage in some secular calling." They will thus have to "tell" people what it means to exist for others, just as Christ was for others. Above all, "our own church [and the emphasis is from Bonhoeffer himself with reference to the Confessing Church] . . . will have to speak of moderation, purity, trust, loyalty, constancy, patience, discipline, humility, contentment, and modesty" (*LPP*, 383).

Bonhoeffer employs the words "say" and "speak" here. That he at the least has other forms of communication in mind is apparent from what follows on the church. "It must not under-estimate the importance of human 'example' (which has its origin in the humanity of Jesus and is so important in Paul's teaching); it is not abstract argument, but example, that gives its word emphasis and power" (*LPP*, 383). It becomes clear that by "doing justice" Bonhoeffer does not have in mind a "deed" or "act" as an exclusive alternative to the word, an ethic that would replace hermeneutics, as if the church should cease to speak of God. Rather his concern is again to lend "emphasis and power" to Christian proclamation. The church's acting restores to the word a portion of its performative character.

I end these initial explorations with three conclusions, on the basis of which I arrive at several questions for treatment in the following chapters.

First, Bonhoeffer's viewpoints on speaking about God, as he formulated them in prison, especially in the baptismal sermon, seem to be severely imbued with an awareness of the deficiencies of Christian speaking about God. Bonhoeffer notes in this respect a fundamental incapacity of the church. He does not situate that in the first place in the inadequacies of language as a means to describe reality. Rather, he looks for the cause in the "pragmatic context" in which God is spoken of. It is a context that is determined by (a) the speakers, who in their personal attitude of faith stand for the truth that they proclaim; (b) the church, which turns speaking about God into one of its own conventions and thus robs itself of the possibility of speaking a different language (that of a "risk for others") than its institutional urge toward self-preservation so that every word spoken from the pulpit is powerless, even before it is spoken; and (c) the culture, which undergoes significant changes so that Christian proclamation runs the risk of becoming unintelligible to people who, "simple as they are," can no longer be religious.

Second, we saw that Bonhoeffer also expressed his faith in the profusion of the Word of God, so that "the world will be changed and renewed by it." His recognition that Christian speaking lags far behind (its deficiency) does not arise out of an insight into the impotence of human speaking about God as such (cf. negative theology), but out of his persistent belief in the power of God's Word. The precariousness of human speaking about God lies for Bonhoeffer in a theology that emanates from a God who speaks, a theology of the Word.

Finally, in the baptismal sermon we encounter Bonhoeffer's recognition of the *limits* of language that characterize both the deficiency and the profusion of speaking about God. Speaking of God requires first of all silence and listening, prayerful listening. It receives power only when supported by doing justice. If Bonhoeffer defends a theology of the Word, it is a theology that does not limit itself to words alone.

The following chapters deal with a number of questions that arise out of these explorations. I do that by allowing the Bonhoeffer from before the letters from prison to speak. I will put questions to him with regard to the deficiency and profusion of speaking about God that have been noted. What conditions have to be met to speak well of God? What are the potentialities and what are the limits of language in this respect? I assume that in the baptismal sermon one finds a crossroads of Bonhoeffer's views on speaking of God. With the help of his earlier theology I attempt to reconstruct the genesis of the baptismal sermon.

I seek a further answer to the following questions: How can someone who is so convinced of the reality-transforming dynamic of the Word of God and so aware of his own incapability still let it resound in a liberating manner? What does Bonhoeffer actually mean by the Word of God and wherein lies its effective power? If Bonhoeffer so exalts the Word of God and, at the same time, so emphasizes the limits of human words, how does he relate the two, divine Word and human word, to each other?

In order to answer these questions chapter three focuses on Bonhoeffer's treatment of human words in general. His family, more than the church, seemed to be his tutor in this case. The careful treatment of words practiced there expressed itself primarily in the art of refraining from words when necessary. Did Bonhoeffer hold that which is true for human words to be the case for the divine as well?

In chapter four I ask what Bonhoeffer meant by the "Word of God," and what according to him makes a word liberating. Was his theology a theology of the Word, like that of Barth? Or did Bonhoeffer have more of an eye for the contextuality of the Word that determines its limits and potentialities?

In chapter five I look into Bonhoeffer's views on church proclamation, particularly as he developed them in the 1930s at Finkenwalde. In the Reformation tradition in which Bonhoeffer stood the sermon is the supreme moment in which God is spoken of, in his commandments and promises. What was Bonhoeffer's position in relation to that tradition? Did the Word of God resound for him only from the pulpit, or elsewhere as well?

In the last chapter I return to the situation of resistance and imprisonment, out of which the baptismal sermon was written, and ask what the significance of that context might be for the development of Bonhoeffer's views on speaking about God. Does it really become impossible in his view to speak a Christian word to another? Or does he only want to strip Christian speech of its supposed self-evidence and bind it to stricter conditions?

3 What Remains Unsaid

The Bonhoeffer Family

Even when one speaks of God, one does so as a human being. How did Bonhoeffer speak as a person, whether he was doing theology or not? It is not always necessary to ask about the person behind the work, the biography behind the theology. In the case of Bonhoeffer, however, such knowledge clarifies a great deal. The work of a man who let the agenda of his theology be determined by the course of his life cannot be interpreted apart from the context of experience in which it arose and to which it was committed. Someone like Bonhoeffer, who was so clearly convinced of the paradoxical deficiency and profusion in speaking the Word of God, must in his personal life have encountered the limits and potentialities of the human word. It will become clear that Bonhoeffer's origins and the course of his life significantly influenced his views on speaking about God.

3.1 How He Spoke with Others

If we want to know how Bonhoeffer spoke, we must ask in what manner he was a partner in conversation. The biography by his friend and pupil Eberhard Bethge, who, more than any other, knew him intensely and closely, begins with a written portrait that attempts to depict Bonhoeffer in his dealings with others. Bethge sketches in a few short sentences first his outward appearance, his figure, the manner in which he moved and clothed himself.

He has inherited the sensitive mouth and the full, but sharply curved lips of his father. Dietrich's smile was very friendly and warm, but you could sometimes see that he enjoyed poking fun. He spoke without any dialect, and his conversation was remarkably fast. In preaching, his speech became heavy, almost hesitant. . . . In conversation he listened very attentively and asked questions in a way that gave the person he was talking to confidence and made him say more than he thought he could. It was unthinkable that Bonhoeffer would deal with a person in a cursory way. He preferred a small gathering to a large party because he was used to devoting himself entirely to the person he was with and identifying with him. Just as he never hurt another person's feelings, he never let anyone hurt his. This made many people think he was haughty. His very manner expressed this clearly. If he was angry, he expressed it in a voice that became softer, not louder. In his family anger was not thought wrong, only indolence. . . . The stronger the emotions ran the more necessary it was to dress them in insignificant words and gestures.[1]

Notable in this portrait and significant for the impression that Bonhoeffer made is the respect that he displayed for his conversation partner. It was a respect, which could at the same time be experienced as distance, that he purposely brought into the contact. Besides Bethge, others in his vicinity confirm that posture in conversation as characteristic of Bonhoeffer. His pupil Otto Dudzus once gave a similar account of "how he spoke with others," but added a noteworthy detail. "He possessed an unbiased and direct, clear manner of addressing people and including them in conversation. Nonetheless he never looked at them directly, but spoke his words alongside them and looked down at the floor or ground." Dudzus interprets this last peculiarity in a positive manner, although he admits that that was not evident to everyone. He wrote that it did not come forth "out of indifference or reservation, but out of his intention of preserving his nonbias and not irritating his conversation partner by his attentiveness or facial expressions."[2]

---

1. Bethge, *Dietrich Bonhoeffer*, xxiii-xxiv.
2. Quoted in Mayer and Zimmerling, *Mensch hinter Mauern*, 21. Cf. on the other hand the comment of Bonhoeffer's twin sister, Sabine Leibholz. "He always turned his gaze fully towards the person to whom he was speaking" (Wolf-Dieter Zimmermann and Ronald Gregor Smith, eds., *I Knew Dietrich Bonhoeffer*, trans. Käthe Gregor Smith (New York: Harper & Row, 1966), 33. Perhaps the intimacy of the family relation explains the difference.

Apparently others experienced Bonhoeffer as a conversation partner who took them completely seriously. Without restraint he was fully present in conversation, but at the same time he never surrendered himself to another person or to the encounter of the moment. While one spoke with him, a great deal remained unsaid, and one was aware of that. For many that must have left the impression of his being closed or reticent. At times that created difficulties in relations with others. Wilhelm Rott, a student of Bonhoeffer who described his teacher as "essentially a man of distance," was surprised when he heard in Finkenwalde that, besides his family members, there was only one person with whom Bonhoeffer spoke in the familiar form of German address. (In the seminary, to be sure, the number increased quickly.)[3] Rott's fellow student Wolf-Dieter Zimmermann speaks openly of the cold, distanced impression that Bonhoeffer made on him, as someone with whom one could seldom experience direct warmth. But he certainly did not conclude that it expressed a haughty will to dominate. On the contrary, Bonhoeffer made on him a lasting impression of one who devoted himself completely to anyone who needed his attention.[4]

Bonhoeffer was conscious of the impression of being reticent that he made on others, as well as the fact that it was not always appreciated. In a letter to Bethge he characterizes his friend as "by nature open and modest, whereas I am reticent and rather demanding" (*LPP*, 189). The friends accepted each other, however, as they were. That cannot be said of his intended family-in-law, the von Wedemeyers. When he wanted to marry the eighteen-year-old Maria von Wedemeyer, daughter of Prussian landed gentry from Pätzig (Pommern), whom he met while at nearby Finkenwalde, he felt that the mother of his fiancée meddled too much in their relationship. Not only did she want the couple to take a year for consideration, she also wished to exercise influence on the character of her son-in-law to be. Bonhoeffer vents his feelings in a letter to Bethge: "There are few

3. Ibid., 132.

4. Wolf-Dieter Zimmermann, *Wir nannten ihn Bruder Bonhoeffer: Einblicke in ein hoffnungsvolles Leben* (We called him Brother Bonhoeffer: Insights into a hopeful life) (Berlin: Wichern, 1995), 47, 77. His sister-in-law Emmi Bonhoeffer writes in Zimmermann and Smith, *I Knew Dietrich Bonhoeffer*, 29: "He himself was one who asked questions. He could not stand empty talk." That Bonhoeffer perceived of himself as being dominant, and suffered under that, is another matter. In Tegel he spoke to Bethge of his "tyrannical nature" (*LPP*, 148), while having already written to him about his "certain act of violence" that he abhorred (letter from February 1, 1941, *GS*, 2:397).

people who know how to value reticence. I think father and mother can. . . . With regard to reticence, it all depends on *what* we are keeping to ourselves, and on whether there is one person with whom we can share everything" (*LPP*, 288; May 7, 1944). The one person who can expect complete openness, is that Bethge to whom the letter is addressed? Or is it Maria about whom the passage is written? It is not clear, although one suspects on the basis of the letters that Bonhoeffer wrote from prison that he probably had Bethge in mind here.[5]

Maria von Wedemeyer also thought that Bonhoeffer was not nearly open enough and kept too much to himself. The more recently published *Love Letters from Cell 92* are a moving document in this respect, marked as they are by the wrestling for understanding of two people who hardly knew each other. Such was their involvement while they were living separated from each other under continual threat of danger to their lives. Maria admitted to Dietrich that she had always willingly told her parents and family members all they wanted to know about her. "I've never made it difficult for them to see into the innermost depths of my heart" (*LL*, 208).[6] In contrast, we can notice from the letters that Bonhoeffer sent her how frugal he wanted to be with words, even if Maria yearned for them. When he commemorates the first anniversary of the death of her father, who fell in 1942, he writes: "Later on, if you wish, you must tell me all about your father and August 22nd. But perhaps you'd rather not. There are many things one cannot speak of" (*LL*, 69). On Christmas Eve, 1943, Maria reads: "This is a time when there's so much to say that silence is the only real answer" (*LL*, 143). That Maria at times thought differently becomes clear when in the following month both came to speak about their quite different literary preferences. She writes her fiancé about a book by

5. Cf. Christian Gremmels, "'Seit Du einmal vor vielen Jahren . . .' Unbekannte Passagen aus den Briefen von Dietrich Bonhoeffer und Eberhard Bethge" ("Since for many years ago you . . ." Unknown fragments from the letters of Dietrich Bonhoeffer to Eberhard Bethge), in C. Gremmels and W. Huber, eds., *Theologie und Freundschaft; Wechselwirkungen: Eberhard Bethge und Dietrich Bonhoeffer* (Theology and friendship; interactions: Eberhard Bethge and Dietrich Bonhoeffer) (Munich: Chr. Kaiser, 1994), 135-53, esp. 138. Gremmels reinserts Bethge's redactional omission (here in italics) in the quotation of a letter from *LPP*, which will also be included in the *DBW* edition of the prison letters. "If you had been there, Eberhard, you *alone* would have done the duty of a friend by telling me the truth" (*LPP*, 172).

6. She does add that since the death of her father and brother, both of whom died on the front, "it has been a different story."

Werner Bergengruen that she recommends to him (*Der spanische Rosen-stock*, 1940) and compares the described relation of the poet and his loved one with that of the two of them. Maria's vehemence betrays more than an artistic difference of insight. "You say that Bergengruen is too explicit for you. You may be right, but you know, there are some stupid people — e.g. your fiancée — who don't understand implicit things and are grateful when they're spelled out. Every book means and conveys something differ-ent to every individual, so it also withholds something different. Anyway, why should those two people have withheld anything from each other? If ever there was a moment to say something frankly and fully, that was it" (*LL*, 194).

For his part Bonhoeffer was greatly annoyed by the advice of his mother-in-law to fill Maria's visits in prison with more content by letting her think up questions ahead of time that Dietrich could answer and by enriching the visits with Bible study and meditation. Bonhoeffer had no desire for such piety, for their encounters had no need of a religious sur-plus. "As if I'm forever eager to engage in profound, intellectual discus-sions! . . . There will be times when we're drawn to fundamentals of our own accord, but God subsists not only in fundamentals but in everyday life as well" (*LL*, 202). In addition Bonhoeffer wanted to know nothing of the openness that such piety presupposes. In the same letter, of March 11, 1944, he writes Maria, "How could I say even to Mother — with a prize gossip sitting in on our conversation! — what I would hesitate to tell even you, because important matters should be reserved for important occa-sions? . . . I neither can nor should tell anyone else what I want to tell you. It belongs to us alone, just you and me. Can you understand that, and do you think as I do? Grandmother [Ruth von Kleist-Retzov] once called me 'reticent,' and I'm afraid that, once voiced, such characterizations stick. What Grandmother means by reticence is that I don't discuss everything, nor do I wish to, even with my intimates. For all the love I bear my parents and brothers and sisters, and for all my close friendship with Grand-mother, there are certain things I don't discuss with them because they're incompatible with the nature of our relationship. Grandmother dislikes that, but she can't, I fear, change it because I consider it the right and proper thing for me personally."[7]

7. On Ruth von Kleist see also Jane Pejsa, *Matriarch of Conspiracy: Ruth von Kleist 1867-1945* (Minneapolis: Kenwood, 1992).

3.2 Naturalness, Tact, and Simplicity
(The Art of Conversation)

Bonhoeffer then made an attempt to place what others call his "reticence" in a proper light for Maria. Almost desperately he did his best to be understood by the woman with whom he wanted to share his life. "I don't believe that the people who really know me, Klaus [Bonhoeffer], Christel [von Dohnanyi], Eberhard [Bethge], not to mention my parents, think me reticent and I am sure, dearest Maria, that you'll one day marvel at how unreticent I am, indeed, how immensely difficult I shall find it to keep things to myself, and how I long to share with you what I have to withhold from others. Most people think me quiet, aloof, even forbidding; you will come to know a different side of me" (*LL*, 202).

That this was not a coincidental characteristic of a silent man but a cultivated manner of an entire family became apparent when Maria decided to go to help Dietrich's parents in Berlin and stay for a time with them. Again Bonhoeffer was uncertain whether Maria would be able properly to appreciate the frugality with words that he and his parents shared. "You must now be trying to acclimatize yourself to everyday life with my parents. I don't think you'll find it too easy from many aspects. They're both extremely fond of you, but it's a fact that such things are hardly ever voiced in our family, whereas in yours they are. There's certainly no point in arguing over which is 'better.' They are different people, and they behave as their inner selves dictate. But I can imagine that you'll find it hard at first to accept that we leave many things unspoken, especially in the religious domain" (*LL*, 262).

It becomes clear that Bonhoeffer by "reticence" is not thinking of silence in general, but rather of silence with regard to intense and intimate feelings, including religious feelings. That does not mean that they are never spoken of. It means that they must first overcome the barrier of certain reservations. Meaningful words are to be preserved for great occasions. "I don't think either of us likes to say much about the things we're finding difficult, but when they threaten to become too difficult, let us always tell each other, quite candidly and confidently, that we not only want to help each other but can really do so." Those are words he writes to Maria on April 16, 1944 (*LL*, 221). Again he seeks to share his feelings with her, but has difficulty conveying to her the caution with which he treats words. One cannot always and everywhere talk about everything with everybody.

That might be a good description of the care with which one in the Bonhoeffer house attended to words. That attitude can also be seen as a well-cultivated inheritance of the family. Just as the Bonhoeffer family carefully cherished the cultural inheritance of former generations, so did each particular member of the family cherish in turn the values and norms of their own upbringing. Not that the Bonhoeffers were family weary. They heartily encouraged and tolerated each going in his or her own direction in life. But it is seldom that family ties have been so enfolded and valued as in this environment, especially in times of crisis and danger, as in the 1930s and 1940s. Every Saturday evening, when they as a family entertained each other with chamber music, can serve as a model of the social intercourse that they were accustomed to practice.[8] The Bonhoeffers did not consider family to be a goal in itself. They had no notion of modern "cocooning," even if the sense of security in the bosom of one's family must certainly have been a comfort to Dietrich in the darkest moments of imprisonment.[9] The family was first of all a sort of practice area, in which one could train oneself in the human relations to which one was called outside the family. "In the long run, human relationships are the most important thing in life." Bonhoeffer writes this to Bethge from prison in describing the experience of the happiness that overcomes him when he can "be for others." "People are more important than anything else in life" (*LPP*, 386). One can trace this family trait to Bonhoeffer's social philosophy and doctrine of the church (as a "church for others"). His own family let Bonhoeffer feel again and again "how our own lives are bound up with other people's, and in fact how the center of our own lives is outside ourselves, and how little we are separate entities" (*LPP*, 105).[10]

The significance of family relations for Bonhoeffer's theology cannot be overestimated. He confessed to Bethge that his education *(Ausbildung)* meant "almost everything" to him (*LPP*, 309). Almost uncritically, Bonhoeffer assumed the values and norms that were wielded in his family, all

8. Cf. *LPP*, 117, 127, 150.

9. The "kindly powers" from the poem bearing the same name are in the first place intended profanely (*LPP*, 400; cf. 73; *LL*, 269-70, 127). Cf. also *LPP*, 119: "But in the last resort, for me at any rate, the 'world' consists of a few people whom I should like to see and to be with."

10. Cf. *LPP*, 150: "I believe that this helping one another is a heritage in which all the members of the family share. . . . The wish to be independent in everything is false pride. Even what we owe to others belongs to ourselves."

the more when they were pressured from outside. The Bonhoeffer house became his general social and moral standard from which he derived criteria for human affairs, particularly and without reserve during the period of imprisonment.

That holds also for his dealings with words. The Bonhoeffers cultivated general middle-class standards as were common among the educated middle class of Berlin at the beginning of the twentieth century. The intellectual games at table, in which their father enjoyed letting the Bonhoeffer children define things and concepts (albeit only when he explicitly invited them to do so, for usually only the parents conversed during the meal while the children kept silent),[11] had their effect in the uneasiness Bonhoeffer felt when someone too easily took refuge in the expression: "There are no words for that." On November 26, 1943, he wrote to Bethge: "I always hesitate to use the word 'indescribable,' because if you take enough trouble to make a thing clear, I think there is very little that is really 'indescribable.'" Bonhoeffer added immediately that the visit he had just received from Bethge, in the company of his parents and his fiancée Maria, belonged to that category (LPP, 145). In a family where every word that was uttered had first to cross a threshold, one probably had to grow accustomed to the spontaneity of a "blabbermouth" like Maria von Wedemeyer. (The Love Letters speak clearly on this.) "I have found it one of the most potent educative factors in our family that we had so many hindrances to overcome (in connection with relevance, clarity, naturalness, tact, simplicity, etc.) before we could express ourselves properly" (LPP, 386-87). In this context Bonhoeffer speaks of "the inconveniences of education," but he does not give the impression that he greatly suffered under it.

Among the Bonhoeffers, words were measured by high standards before they could be spoken. But what were the demands that had to be met? It seems that the Bonhoeffer family clearly deviated from other families of the same professorial environment of Berlin. Bonhoeffer mentioned naturalness, tact, and simplicity as standards by which one measured what was said. There was a preference for manners that were authentic, unbiased, and unsophisticated. The "middle-class pride" expressed in the parents' refusal to decorate their children with "extrava-

11. Sabine Leibholz-Bonhoeffer, quoted in Zimmermann and Smith, *I Knew Dietrich Bonhoeffer*, 22.

WHAT REMAINS UNSAID | 47

gant" names was exemplary of the basic attitude of "Act normal. That's crazy enough" (*FP*, 59). In that context the experience of a girl next door, Emmi Delbrück (daughter of the historian Hans Delbrück and the later wife of Dietrich's brother Klaus), on the occasion of her first aquaintance with the Bonhoeffer family, was very telling. "All the Bonhoeffers reacted with extreme sensitivity against every mannerism and affectation of thought; I think it was in their nature, and sharpened by their education. They were allergic to even the slightest touch of this, it made them intolerant, even unjust. Whereas we Delbrücks shrank from saying anything banal, the Bonhoeffers shrank from saying anything interesting for fear it might turn out to be not so interesting after all, and the inherent claim might be ironically smiled at."[12]

Emmi Delbrück-Bonhoeffer adds that the father, Karl Bonhoeffer, was especially accustomed to ridiculing such ostentatiousness. That is in line with the lasting impression that his personality made on his son Dietrich (cf. 3.3). In the presence of Karl Bonhoeffer one kept quiet, rather than run the risk of chattering impertinently. In his fatherly authority he understood at the same time the art of taking the most stupid questions of his children seriously and answering them matter-of-factly. Nevertheless the predominant impression that Emmi Bonhoeffer described remains. "In the Bonhoeffer family one learnt to think before asking a question or making a remark."[13] That could result in a compulsive reticence if the words were to be weighed according to their intellectual weight. But that was not the case. What one said did not have to be "interesting" so long as it was expressed with naturalness, tact, and simplicity. Weighing one's words did not hinder one from speaking frankly and freely. On the contrary, it required such directness. If one tried too hard to impress others, one made a bad impression.[14]

12. Quoted in Zimmermann and Smith, *I Knew Dietrich Bonhoeffer*, 36.
13. Ibid.
14. Cf. the description of Bonhoeffer's alter ego Christoph in the novel that he wrote in prison. "These candid words and the upright attitude of the seventeen year-old who stood in front of the major without embarrassment . . . compared favorably with the false smile of the young man in full-dress uniform" (*FP*, 81).

3.3 The Aversion to the "Phraseological" (Karl Bonhoeffer)

In the Bonhoeffer family father Karl was held to be the person from whom one could best learn what to say and what to leave unsaid.[15] The lasting impression that he made on his son Dietrich has already been mentioned. In a letter to Bethge from prison Dietrich asks himself whether in the course of his life he has changed as a person. "I do not think that I have ever changed very much, except perhaps at the time of my first impressions abroad and under the first conscious influence of father's personality. It was then that I turned from phraseology to reality" (*LPP*, 275). Whether, when, and how that "turn" might be traced in Bonhoeffer's theological writings is a question I will not answer here (although one can observe a conspicuous difference in style between his early writings, written in a difficult and learned professorial German, as well as the flowery and at times pathetic style of his first sermons, on the one hand, and on the other hand, his writings and sermons from 1930 on that employ a much more accessible and lucid language). At any rate Karl Bonhoeffer definitely left his stamp on his son's use of words.[16] In descriptions of his personality, his "taciturn" character turns up again and again. In her remembrances of her father, Dietrich's twin sister Sabine mentions "his controlled temperament" that did not permit him to speak a thoughtless word. "His rejection of hollow phrases may have made us at times tongue-tied and uneasy, but as a result we could not abide any clichés, gossip, platitudes or pomposity when we grew up."[17] If Karl Bonhoeffer wanted to emphasize what he was saying, Sabine notes, then he did so not by raising his voice but by accentuating his words. His

---

15. Cf. *FP*, 59, on "the grandmother, who knew how to keep quiet."

16. Cf. *FP*, 61: "A reply to the statement of his father, who was his absolute standard for everything, was out of the question for Christoph." That not only his father but also Adolf von Harnack played a formative role in Bonhoeffer's frugal manner with words can be concluded from Bonhoeffer's commemoration at Harnack's funeral. Bonhoeffer characterized him as preeminently a theologian, "one who speaks of God." He then commented, "It was of his nature to say only a little in this respect. He would rather say far too few words than one word too much on such matters. Everything had to be done with integrity and simplicity. But the little that he had to say . . . was enough for us" (*GS*, 3:61).

17. Quoted in Zimmermann and Smith, *I Knew Dietrich Bonhoeffer*, 22.

closest colleagues in the psychiatric clinic in Berlin also remembered the psychiatrist Karl Bonhoeffer as a cautious man of few words. "Not much was said, at least nothing superfluous. . . . Any superfluous chatter fell silent in his presence. He had no use for poorly supported speculations and theoretical exaggerations, or for exaggerated or misplaced pathos and inflated, fashionable terminology. . . . From no one could one learn better that silence is an important form of speaking."[18]

A lack of words was, however, compensated by his expressiveness. Karl Bonhoeffer spoke a great deal but differently. Nowhere is the rather silent man pictured as a recluse. On the contrary, his social presence was emphatic. In family circles one especially remembered his eyes, which could look right through you.[19] Even when there was no verbal communication, a transfer of meaning was still enacted. "Words do not play a big role, one understands the look, the gesture," as Bonhoeffer writes down in a scribble intended for the drama that he wants to write in prison. He thus indicates how much attention was paid to nonverbal communication in family circles.[20] The silence at issue here, of which Karl Bonhoeffer was the great example, was not experienced as speechlessness, an encounter with the limits of what humans can meaningfully exchange, but rather as a silence at the service of language. It was another form of speaking, perhaps more subtle, but not less communicative.

The frugality with words is also evident in Bonhoeffer's later literary preferences. Examples are his special liking for the writings of Georges Bernanos, of which he writes in 1940: "When minister say something from them, then their words carry weight." The weight of a word is dependent on the depth out of which it arises (*GS*, 3:43). There is also his admiration for Ernest Hello, who wrote: "In deeply moved silence language rises to its greatest blossoming." His admiration for Adalbert Stifter increased while in prison, because as a writer Stifter refused in his descriptions to intrude into people's inner life, thus respecting one's privacy (*LPP*, 158, 162). Such

18. J. Zutt, quoted in the German edition of Bethge's biography *(Dietrich Bonhoeffer: Theologe, Christ, Zeitgenosse* [Munich: Chr. Kaiser, 1967], 638). In this context one can also point to the businesslike style, with once in a while an understatement (such as the comment on the film that they wanted to make of him in *LPP*, 51), in the letters of father to son in *LPP*.

19. Emmi Bonhoeffer, "The House on Wangenheimstrasse," in *FP*, 133-38, esp. 135.

20. *Fragmente aus Tegel* (German ed. of *Fiction from Prison*), *DBW*, 7, ed. Renate Bethge and Ilse Tödt (Munich: Chr. Kaiser, 1994), 252.

inclinations are unthinkable without Bonhoeffer's education in the language of silence.[21]

In a moving letter, written from prison to Maria von Wedemeyer, it becomes apparent how Bonhoeffer in his relationship with his fiancée had to appeal to this insight into the limits of words, since they could see each other and speak with one another so little. Letters were almost the only route of contact. "I've never sensed such an utter inability to express on paper what I feel about all that has happened to us in the past year. Besides, it may be far from good when all that is usually imparted in silence has to be translated into words. The discrepancy between the reality one desires and the words that aspire to the bridge to that reality, but fail to become so, is too overwhelming" (LL, 161; January 14, 1944). Bonhoeffer imagines meeting Maria at her home and does not suppose that he would exhaust himself with words of happiness and thankfulness. "Were I to see you and come to meet you, would I contrive to utter some words of gratitude for your being there for me, or wouldn't our very nearness speak a wordless language so overpowering that everything else would seem feeble and insubstantial by comparison." In the following sentence he generalizes this experience: "When reality assails my soul too strongly, I become verbally breathless and feel that words would only weaken, disturb and agitate what is strong, lucid and serene" (LL, 162).

Silence for Bonhoeffer did not mean the end of communication but its continuation with other means. A cautious word stood at the service of the art of conversation, which, as was usual in educated circles, was highly regarded among the Bonhoeffers. The ability to carry on a good conversation was a requirement in those intellectual circles. In prison Bonhoeffer realized more clearly than ever that one had to have been brought up in such conversation. He noticed that most people were not capable of carrying on a conversation that transcended their personal matters into a "meeting of minds" (LPP, 213). In the drama fragment that Bonhoeffer wrote in Tegel, he introduces Heinrich, the son of a common laborer, who at home did not learn such an art, through which the talent of friendship can be developed. He experiences such conversation, in which the person-

---

21. The last fifteen years of modern literature Bonhoeffer disdains as "weak lemonade," devoid of clarity and substance. It is characterized by "almost always bad, unfree writing" (LPP, 148-49; cf. 190). For more on Bonhoeffer's views on literature see Wendel, Studien, 196ff.

ality of the conversation partners is the sole condition for conversing, as a requirement that he cannot fulfill. Christoph, in whom one can recognize Bonhoeffer's alter ego, wants to speak with Heinrich personally. Heinrich responds: "Person to person — you always say that when you want to silence the voice of the masses, of the common people, that lives in us. You dislike this voice; you want to rip us out of the community in which alone we are something, and you know perfectly well that you needn't fear us any longer once you confront us as individuals. As individuals we are completely powerless in your hands — for we aren't individuals, we are masses or nothing. Person to person? Let us become persons first, then we'll talk with you person to person" (*FP*, 44). As one gathers from this passage, Bonhoeffer must have often experienced that people who did not share his cultural heritage felt inferior in conversations with him. Not only because they knew less than he (for we saw that the Bonhoeffers had a contempt for intellectualism), but because they were less certain of themselves and their personal identity. They were not familiar with the directness and self-assuredness with which he grew up.[22]

3.4 What Remains Unsaid
(Religious Humanism)

The custom of good conversation became in prison a desire that could seldom be satisfied. After a year of hardly being able to carry on such conversations, Dietrich recognized that he yearned for them. He confessed to Bethge, "I would certainly like to have a good talk with someone, but aimless gossip gets on my nerves terribly" (*LPP*, 271).[23] A good conversation had to be about something for the Bonhoeffers to consider it worthwhile.

22. In the first version of this passage Bonhoeffer has Heinrich say, "You just want to switch the parts, that is all. We can only talk from person to person when we again accept the unselfconscious and the spontaneous deed of the other without suspicion" (*FP*, 182n.49). From the fact that this passage was rewritten three times we may conclude how seriously this experience of exclusion weighed on Bonhoeffer. He lets Christoph say, "I know what kind of quiet strength there is in a good patrician home" (*FP*, 44).

23. Cf. *LPP*, 178: "in spite of all my privations I've come to love solitude. I very much like to talk with two or three people, but I detest anything like a large assembly, and above all any chatter or gossip." Bonhoeffer's claim that "Maria will not have an easy time with me in that respect," we can understand all the better in light of what has been said before.

When is such a conversation worthwhile? For an answer we can turn to the *Fiction from Prison*. In a literary attempt by Bonhoeffer from prison, he compensated his lack of good conversation with fictional exchanges that he let his figures carry on with each other. The drama as well as the novel consist for the most part of dialogues, conversations as, one may assume, had taken place in the Bonhoeffer family.[24] Some conversations are about the art of conversation. "There are conversations in which the partners challenge each other; other conversations are like violent explorations; still others are noncommital chats that barely veil the distance, the strangeness, and the indifference between people. But when a conversation is mutually giving and receiving there is neither violence nor indifference" (*FP*, 94). Such conversation, in which openness and trust between the conversation partners is not at the expense of the freedom afforded each other, is what Bonhoeffer calls a "good" conversation.

The dialogue that he then attributes in his novel to Christoph and his loved one Renate is a good example of that. Bonhoeffer presents their dialogue as an effortlessly unfolding conversation that seems to carry the speakers along on its rhythm. "They didn't question each other; what each wanted to say of one's life, one's views, one's closest friends, was to be said freely. In this way one of those rare and happy conversations came about in which each word is taken as the free gift of the one to the other. . . . It is a slow, free process of mutual bonding" (*FP*, 94).[25] A good conversation requires a deepening of the relation between the conversation partners and the exploration of their personalities. In such dialogue people help reveal each other's humanity. The word "gift" is significant in this context. "Being with and for each other" in conversation is a sort of secular experience of grace. Without others, as I already quoted Bonhoeffer, a person is nothing and nobody. Language seems consequently to be for him more than a mere instrument. It is a communicative medium in which the heart of being human is revealed. We are nothing, but in speaking we become someone for others. Conversation is a locus of anthropological "revelation," in which people mutually bestow to each other their essence. In this context we read that "when a conversation is mutually giving and receiving there is neither

24. According to Renate and Eberhard Bethge in their introduction to *FP*, 5.
25. A variant that Bonhoeffer marked out is more flowery: "Out of the freely flowering word of the one, the magic wand . . . springs the words of the other who opens up the pure source of the word in the other" (*FP*, 191n.112).

violence nor indifference. The unspoken remnant is a hint of undiscovered treasures of still concealed wealth in the other which will reveal itself at a given hour" (*FP*, 94).

"The unspoken remnant" is a significant phrase in which the direct link between Bonhoeffer's views on speaking and silence on the one hand, and his views on humanity on the other hand, are concentrated. It is the same intuition that he expressed ten years earlier in the language of Christology, that no person is present or given in advance to another, but that each person eludes the grip that is placed on him or her by use of labels.[26] People really encounter each other in a relationship of disclosure and concealment that can in no way be manipulated. The inviolable secret of each person manifests itself in that which is not said, precisely in the fact that it cannot be forced out of them. Almost all reflections on language (and its limits) in Bonhoeffer's writings are placed in this metaphysical-anthropological framework.

I return to the concept of "secret" later on (see 4.5). Here I note that for him the upper-middle-class "art of conversation" meant more than just courteousness and a lifestyle. For him conversation was a place where humanity reveals itself. The cautiousness and the reticence that he observed are to be seen as more than a psychological or characteristic peculiarity. For Bonhoeffer an entire metaphysics and ethics were at stake.

I can illustrate this again with a passage from the drama fragment on which Bonhoeffer worked in Tegel before he began work on a novel. Here also we encounter a Christoph and a Renate, but the first is doomed to death as a result of having been wounded on the front lines. Does he know that himself or not? His fiancée Renate and his friend Ulrich find it difficult to see what is going on inside him. Renate is of the opinion that at the moment "both of us simply have to be here for him, without wanting to press or influence him. He must simply know that we are present for him" (*FP*, 31). Ulrich finds it difficult to agree to that. They have never concealed anything from each other. Why now? He does not like playing hide-and-seek among friends. Renate answers him, "Even friends, yes, even husband and wife, can't always tell each other everything. They must sometimes wait for one another for a long time till the first word has grown and rip-

---

26. *Christ the Center (CC)*, translation of the lectures on Christology, 1933. Christ is spoken of as the "Logos," the speaking other. But as Word he is unutterable, so that only silence is fitting in his presence. See 4.5.

ened. Words have their time. Words forced out of you are like torn-off buds. . . . Sometimes there are things about which one must keep silent for a while before one can say them, even among friends and between husband and wife. One must give the other time. Openness is something very beautiful, but it's even more important to be open to the other, to his silence too" (*FP*, 31-32). Ulrich is not so easily convinced, however, and pleads for clarity and transparency in their friendship. Again Renate attempts to change his mind. "What does that mean? Do you want to see him like a photograph which registers everything, or with eyes that respectfully and lovingly perceive and receive the essential picture of the other, eyes that allow the other his secret?" (*FP*, 32).

Again we encounter the word "secret," once again at the cutting edge of speaking and remaining silent, where the metaphysical heart, the "essential picture," of humanity reveals itself. But this time Renate goes even further and pushes through to the point where the existential heart of Bonhoeffer's theology beats. When Ulrich still does not want to give in and comments that a person can also perish by keeping a secret (he prefers to inform Christoph of his fate), Bonhoeffer lets Renate speak the following words, from which it becomes apparent that Bonhoeffer understands "secret" to mean more than an amount of information that is not yet known. "And yet one may steal nobody's secret without destroying him. Did you never sense that especially the very good people we know carry a secret which never reveals itself and which they themselves do not dare to touch? It shines through every word, through every glance of these people. But if you wanted to tell it, the best would be ruined. . . . The last secret of every human being is God; that we must let him have" (*FP*, 32).[27] The human secret, which for Bonhoeffer is here identical with the religious mystery, is apparently not something that can be disclosed so that we might "know" it and "say" what it is. It is not a riddle that can be solved. It is not something that can be expressed in terms of knowledge and made available. Even though it is always present as it shines through every word and through every glance, it remains absent, precisely in the elusive manner in which it is

---

27. Again the lectures on Christology provide a parallel. The dialogue in which the secret of another person is not respected but demanded of him is that between Pilate and Jesus. "Man seeks to deny the one with whom he is confronted. Pilate asks, 'Who are you?' and Jesus is silent. Man cannot wait for the answer, because it is too dangerous. The logos cannot endure the Counter-Logos. It knows that one of them must die and it therefore kills the one whom it asks" (*CC*, 33).

present. The person who has it does not have it as a possession at his or her disposal. From this theological perspective it becomes clear what great value Bonhoeffer attributed to a good conversation. The upper-middle-class art of conversation that was exercised in the Bonhoeffer family possessed for him an additional metaphysical value. In conversation the hidden structures of human existence are uncovered.

The reticence in conversation that was advocated by the Bonhoeffers might also be interpreted solely in terms of a Protestant, middle-class asceticism, as an expression of self-control and the rational capacity to master one's elementary impulses. Of course, it was that as well. In prison Bonhoeffer wrote a poem in which self-control (discipline of the "senses and soul") is viewed as a necessary stage on the road to freedom.[28] A person who is not capable of such asceticism and who ventilates his or her feelings to anybody and everybody is a chatterer, of whom Bonhoeffer has nothing nice to say. In women he perhaps considers it charming (!); in men he finds it quite repugnant (*LPP*, 212-13; February 13, 1944). He complains to Bethge about the almost sickly "need to be communicative" of some of his fellow prisoners in Tegel. "There is quite indiscriminate gossip, in front of all comers, about one's own affairs, no matter whether they interest or concern other people or not, simply, in fact, because one just has to gossip." Bonhoeffer is glad that he has learned to suppress his inclinations. "It's an almost physical urge, but if you manage to suppress it for a few hours, you're glad afterwards that you didn't let yourself go" (ibid.). In that respect, one could dispense with Bonhoeffer's attitude as being typically upper middle class.

The matter of self-control becomes noteworthy, however, due to the ethical context in which Bonhoeffer places it. It serves as a function, and that is a second interpretation, of respect for one another. In the drama fragment from Tegel we can read that people "don't exist to look into the depths of each other's hearts" (*FP*, 45). Here Bonhoeffer again takes up the line of his yet unfinished *Ethics*, in which he made a plea for shame, understood as a moral virtue that respects the limits of the personal sphere of life. People are not supposed to expose themselves and others unashamedly to the unbridled expression of their own impulses. Bonhoeffer wrote: "Nor will the most profound and intimate joy or grief allow itself to be dis-

---

28. "For the secret of freedom no one discovers, without rigorous disciplining of self" (*LPP*, 371, translation from *TF*, 516).

closed in words" (*E*, 7-8). How shame can be of concrete moral importance Bonhoeffer discovered during the many bomb alarms in prison, when people spoke of their fears openly. He perceived it as something disarming on the one hand, while on the other hand as a sort of cynical obscenity (*LPP*, 146; November 11, 1943). Not only does one relinquish one's independence by fully surrendering oneself to others; one also burdens the relation with others with a weight that the other probably cannot bear. One may not inflict others, including the relationship that one has with them, however intimate, with such openness (*E*, 8). Bonhoeffer is of the opinion that such openness is only fitting in the relation that people maintain with God. It can at the most be practiced in confession (*LPP*, 159; December 5, 1943). In a further passage of his novel we read: "There must be a point to it . . . that the inner life of another is by nature inaccessible to us, and that no one can see into our inner being. We must obviously be meant to keep it for ourselves and not share it with another." To those words of Christoph his friend Ulrich responds after a long silence: "Except with God — or with a human being given to us by God, who can keep as silent as God does" (*FP*, 92).[29]

One also finds in Bonhoeffer's writings a moral reason to be sparing with words. He considers not only idle chatter to be reprehensible but gossip as well. In Finkenwalde he introduced the rule that one was not allowed to express a judgment on someone else except in his presence. It entails a "discipline of the tongue" of which the ethical concern is clear enough, but for which the motivation is noteworthy and typical of Bonhoeffer, namely, the conviction that "we combat our evil thoughts most effectively when we absolutely refuse to allow them to be verbalized" (*LT*, 94).[30] This conscientious usage of words, which Bonhoeffer had learned in his parental home,

---

29. On confession see especially the lectures on spiritual care, 1935-1939 (*Spiritual Care*, translated and with an introduction by Jay C. Rochelle [Philadelphia: Fortress Press, 1985]). See also *LT*, 108-18. Confession can in turn degenerate into a pious achievement. "If they do so, it will become the worst, most abominable, unholy and unchaste betrayal of the heart. Confession then becomes sensual prattle" (*LT*, 116). For more references and an analysis of the meaning of confession for Bonhoeffer, see H. R. Pelikan, *Die Frömmigkeit Dietrich Bonhoeffers: Äußerungen, Grundlinien, Entwicklung* (The spirituality of Dietrich Bonhoeffer: Expressions, patterns, development) (Vienna: Herder, 1981), 161ff.

30. "It is just as certain that the individual judgmental thought can be limited and suppressed by never allowing it to be spoken except as a confession of sin" (*LT*, 94).

was something that he wanted to pass on to his students as a Christian virtue.[31]

3.5 Pious Chatter (Experiences as a Youth in the Church)

In the above consideration of the Christian humanistic dimensions of language, the role of Christian faith is not explicit. Only once did we hear Bonhoeffer say to Maria von Wedemeyer that in his family, in contrast to hers, much remained unsaid, "especially in the religious domain" (*LL*, 262). That is in line with what we had already heard in the baptismal sermon about the piety of his parental home, which was not "noisy or loquacious." That the Bonhoeffers were not very churchgoing and did not display their Christianity is well known. They would likely have wanted to describe themselves as being "Protestant" and "Christian," but they certainly did not exert themselves to let that be noticeable. Dietrich Bonhoeffer's choice of theology was no natural occurrence. Indeed, the male members of his family sought to dissuade him from beginning a career in that "boring, lower middle-class, weakly institution" of the Lutheran Church. Bethge's biography emphasizes the rather cool relation that existed between the official church and the enlightened, liberal environment of the Bonhoeffers.[32] Bethge speaks of a "subdued respect." Here I limit myself to the question of what role the usage of words that was practiced by the Bonhoeffers on the one hand, and by the church on the other hand, played in the distance that they maintained toward the church.

We have seen how among the Bonhoeffers, words blossomed the most in personal dialogue. Does not the fact that in church someone always held a monologue from the pulpit explain in part the family's dislike for churchy sermons? Karl Bonhoeffer, a man of few words, expressed it literally, when accounting for the fact that he had not wanted to become a minister like several of his forefathers, stating that it was due to his "pronounced aversion to speak alone every Sunday."[33] "Damned monologues!"

---

31. Zimmermann, *Bruder Bonhoeffer*, 77.

32. Bethge, *Dietrich Bonhoeffer*, 20ff. Cf. also my *Grond onder de voeten*, 90ff.

33. Karl Bonhoeffer, "Lebenserinnerungen: Geschrieben für die Familie" (Memories: Written for the family), in *Karl Bonhoeffer zum Hundertsten Geburtstag am 31 März*

were the words that Dietrich Bonhoeffer put in the mouth of his alter ego Christoph in the drama fragment from Tegel, whereupon Christoph sought conversation with Heinrich, a person who was for him totally different and unfamiliar (*FP*, 31).

We also observed how readily Bonhoeffer described the intimacy of dialogue in terms of a "dialectic of concealment and exposure" (*E*, 8). Precisely in the tension between silence and speaking, the secret of humanity is revealed. That "religious humanism" constituted a sort of secular religion within the Bonhoeffer family, even if it was only enunciated in that way by the theologian Bonhoeffer. Was this belief in the religious mystery of a personal word not contrary to the emphatically public character of church proclamation? Or to put it in the words of Renate in the aforementioned drama fragment, a word cannot grow in the pulpit. There is no room for patiently awaiting the moment that it ripens. It has, as a matter of necessity, to be "plucked in bud." The language of the pulpit is the language of institutional proclamation. It does not allow one to wait for the redeeming word. "You cannot always and everywhere talk about everything with everybody." Such was the characterization I gave to the position with which the Bonhoeffers were brought up (3.2). Time, place, conversation partners, topics of conversation — the redeeming is dependent on situation and context. In that context the proclamation of the church must have been experienced as a "great word," which was spoken even when there was no "great moment."

The opening of the novel from prison is quite telling on the disappointing experience of the Bonhoeffer family with regard to preaching in the church (*FP*, 49ff.). Bonhoeffer's description is similar to what he experienced as a young person when he visited the church in Berlin-Grunewald.[34] It is Sunday and the elderly Frau Karoline Brake comes out of the church. On the way home the decline of culture and the decay of tradition concern her. The restfulness of the Sunday is trampled upon, and the "fear of silence" that is evident from the noisy behavior of young people is a sign of general decline. But is the church not a beacon, a stronghold in the crisis of a culture that is no longer fluent in the language of silence? On the contrary, the wife of the former mayor has just heard "a miserable

---

1968 (On the occasion of Karl Bonhoeffer's centennial birthday on March 31, 1968), ed. J. Zutt et al. (Berlin: Springer Verlag, 1969), 8-107, esp. 20.

34. *FP*, 185n.11.

sermon" that only arouses anger in her. "The nonsense she had been subjected to! Could one blame her children and grandchildren for always letting her go to church alone?" She agreed with her grandson, who said that
he had grown out of such "preacher wisdom." He said to her: "Grandmother, . . . I really don't understand how you can listen to it Sunday after
Sunday." She had answered that what mattered was not whether you always heard something new in the sermon, but whether something good
was said. Well, this Sunday she had not heard anything new, but nothing
good either. Did Christianity with its present-day representatives amount
to anything? She was not so sure, in light of the quality of the preaching.
"It was nonsense, and for her that was the worst thing there could be from
the pulpit." To be sure: "Every bad sermon was a nail in the coffin of Christian faith. One could not deny it anymore: Here in this suburb, at least, the
word of God had turned into nonsense" (*FP*, 50-51).

The resolute woman, with characteristics of both Dietrich's grandmother Julie Bonhoeffer and Ruth von Kleist-Retzov, Maria von Wedemeyer's grandmother and a faithful ally of the Confessing Church, does
not, however, want to let things be. "She would see to it that this old sweet-
talker disappeared from the pulpit, or else that a second minister, a
preacher of the word of God, was engaged" (*FP*, 52). All of her attempts to
change his ways became stranded on his vanity and his idle sense of ministry. Since then he avoided her, because, as she was convinced, he was afraid
of her. She still attended his services, although she no longer hoped to hear
his mouth utter the Word of God. But now she was fed up. "It wasn't for
her personally; she had learned during the years how to ignore the babble
and to hold on to the few words containing truth." She would have been
able to persevere for the rest of her life. But now what mattered was not
herself but the parish. "The congregation, the whole town, her own family
were left without the word of God, and that meant, sooner or later, that all
of life had to lose its orientation" (*FP*, 52). Might it be God's judgment to
deprive this generation of the Word? Nevertheless, she would "take God by
God's Word and not let go, unless God blessed her" (*FP*, 52).

It astonishes Frau Brake that she is practically the only one who complains about the quality of the preaching. The only other one to complain
is the custodian, which indicates that the preaching is not being measured
by an intellectual or cultural standard and that the recognition of human
quality is not bound to social position (cf. *LPP*, 12-13). In the proclamation of that morning she had heard nothing but "empty declamations and

cheap phrases." But the cultural elite failed in its judgment. "Why do the 'educated' people, especially, fail so completely in their judgment?" asks Frau Brake. If the value of words is cultivated anywhere at all, then certainly among the educated. In the light of what we have already seen, we can well understand her indignation. "Of course, they hardly ever went to church, but if they had to go to a baptism or a wedding then they always thought the speech — that's what they called the sermon — very nice, very artistic, very modern, very relevant" (*FP*, 53).

Her neighbor, the "Director Warmblut's widow," whom she met on her way home that Sunday morning, is living evidence of the self-deception of the middle class. In the dialogue between Frau Brake and her neighbor, the directress sounds the praises of the morning's sermon, exalting "dear God," the "dear church," and the "dear minister, who can make such human, relevant, and beautiful speeches." Grandmother Brake, however, shares with her neighbor her opposite conviction, "that the minister preached what the congregation wanted to hear, but not the word of God." With even greater indignation she continues her way home. "This pious chatter has nothing to do with Christianity; it is more dangerous than outright disbelief" (*FP*, 54-55).

Her judgment has not yet been tried enough. Upon arriving home, her own maid also ventilates to her the merits of the preacher and his sermons! Just in the way he leans across the pulpit and reaches out with his arms, you can see that "he feels really at home in the pulpit." You can see that he is a man with feeling, quite exalted. He makes one realize that one is living in the suburb of a big town. "In our village the minister was so different, he always spoke evenly and only about the Bible and so on" (*FP*, 56).

From these last remarks it becomes apparent that Bonhoeffer is reproducing more than his experiences as a young person. In Bonhoeffer's description there is also a glimmer of dialectical theology in the line of Barth, who rediscovered the proclamation of the Word and bound it again to the Bible, as a protest against nineteenth-century liberal theology that focused on the exaltation of religious sentimentality. That confrontation, which was for Bonhoeffer to be settled to the advantage of dialectical theology, left its mark on Bonhoeffer's years as a student. For the rest, the novel fragment is relatively devoid of theology. In the standard of measurement that distinguishes between good and bad preaching we recognize the standards maintained in the Bonhoeffer family more than the theology of Barth. The criteria are those by which common human words are tried and tested: tact, simplicity, and authenticity, as opposed to exaggeration and extravagance. Those are the considered requirements that the proclamation of the Word has to satisfy. There is no room for rhetorical tricks, sentimental exhibitionism, or exploitation of feelings. One would then prefer a preacher "who always spoke evenly and only about the Bible and so on."

It is as though Bonhoeffer seeks to describe himself with those last words. He was everything except a gifted preacher, and he never filled the pews. He had a somewhat hesitant delivery with a voice that seemed to get caught in his throat. When his catechism students heard him preach in the Zion Church in Berlin, they concluded spontaneously, "We don't want him here as a preacher. He pauses so much that it's as if he doesn't know what he wants to say!"[35] Bonhoeffer was a preacher who did not search for material in flowery language or emphatic diction, but in the text of the Bible, which he sought to explain in a simple style with a singular well-chosen image.

Did Bonhoeffer expect that his own proclamation could satisfy the conditions that he had learned to place on the spoken word at home? In 1941 when he heard that a member of the family had received the message that he only had a half year to live, Bonhoeffer asked himself what he would do if he were to receive such news. "I think that I would try to teach theology and preach often, just as before" (GS, 6:523). One might say that at that time he had not yet written the baptismal sermon, in which he so sharply exposed the powerlessness of Christian proclamation, and that he had not yet composed the novel in which he parodied the preaching in the church. But even when he had written them, he kept believing in the worth of proclamation. On the day of his death, he held a service of worship for his fellow prisoners, read from the Bible, and preached.[36] Apparently we encounter here a constant element of his work, a fundamental conviction that he carried until the end, that in the Word of God much more is hidden that cannot be dissolved by the deficit of human words. In 1932 he had written, "We do not suffer from the fact that there is too much preaching, but that there is too much bad preaching" (GS, 3:288). We now have an idea what Bonhoeffer meant by

35. Wendel, *Studien*, 20. Cf. Zimmermann and Smith, *I Knew Dietrich Bonhoeffer*, 55; and Bethge's introduction, *GS*, 4:7-8.
36. Bethge, *Dietrich Bonhoeffer*, 1036ff.

"bad preaching." I have to devote another chapter to the question what he meant by good preaching. But first comes a more primary question: What is that which we call the Word of God?

4 Deus Dixit

The Profusion of the Word of God

In a letter, probably from the spring of 1940, Bonhoeffer responds to the judgment of a woman who has written him that the present-day church completely fails to live up to its claims and is in need of a total reformation. The letter in which that judgment was expressed has been lost, so that we cannot be certain what the criticism was to which Bonhoeffer responds. From his "letter to an unknown woman" (who later proved to be Ruth Roberta Heckscher, the oldest daughter of Spes von Kleist), it becomes at least clear what the background of the criticism was, as well as the direction in which the writer sought a solution.

From Bonhoeffer's answer one can notice that he directs his words to someone who shares his social background and who like some of his family is annoyed by the lower-middle-class narrow-mindedness of many church people. But is that lack of education the cause of the fact that the church does not meet the demands of the time, and does its rescue depend on overcoming its cultural arrears by means of a new creative impulse in liturgy and the spoken word? The letter writer seems to have suggested that to Bonhoeffer, but at the very beginning of his letter he states that he must disappoint her in that respect. In the first place, the reformation of the church is not our business, but God's. Furthermore, the only measure of good and bad in the church is Christ himself, not any cultural backwardness. The woman was apparently especially annoyed by the poor quality of church music and liturgy. Bonhoeffer responds that they are to be measured not by aesthetic criteria but by theological ones. "Theological" is to be taken here in the most literal sense of the word, as pertaining to the Word of God. "Again it is more the tenacious concentration on the matter itself, on the Word of God and on Holy Scriptures, that cause something to appear to us to be 'beautiful' or 'ugly'" (GS, 3:39). In that respect, according to Bonhoeffer, the despised and the humble among whom the church arose often have a finer nose than the "educated," to whom the letter writer and Bonhoeffer belong. The cultural elite often fail when it comes to steadfastness or to an act of love or simple prayer. It is better to have bad taste and to know what counts as a Christian, than inversely to have good taste but to miss the decisive heart of Christian faith. In that context, Bonhoeffer is annoyed by those preachers who passionately exploit the sentiments of their audiences, such as he parodied in his fragments for a novel. Even worse for Bonhoeffer is the "educated" preacher, who looks down on all that and thinks to avoid the pitfall by entertaining his congregation "with his 'erudition' rather than with the gospel of Jesus Christ" (GS, 3:41).

4.1 The Depth and the Weight of a Word

In that context Bonhoeffer deals extensively with the problem of the language of proclamation. What he lets the letter writer know is of great importance for our topic. It is characteristic of Bonhoeffer's views on speaking about God in the proclamation of the church.

> You reduce the whole problem to language, and I believe that you are right in doing so. Nowhere is my embarrassment in answering you greater than at this point. Language in the Protestant church, which is a church of the proclamation of God's Word, is no outward matter. I understand well that you are irritated again and again that we pronounce such great and ultimate things, which a person can otherwise hardly utter, as if they were daily matters to be taken for granted. You are certainly right when you say that words like "sin," "grace," "forgiveness," and so on sound totally different and take on a totally different importance when spoken by a person who does not otherwise utter the word. A word that arises out of a prolonged silence before coming to the light has more gravity than the same word out of the mouth of a chatterer. I agree with you, furthermore, that some words we should no longer use, because they are worn out. It has been said time and again that there should be less preaching, in order to lend more emphasis to the words. (GS, 3:41-42)

In this judgment on preaching in the church we fully recognize the son of Karl Bonhoeffer, who taught that a word receives weight only when one has first cherished it inwardly as a precious gem before surrendering it to disclosure. One cannot always and everywhere speak about everything, certainly not about God. This was learned in the Bonhoeffer house. Having become a theologian, Dietrich Bonhoeffer is apparently willing to measure speaking about God by the same standards of frugality with words and the scruple that a great word demands a great moment.

Does the weekly sermon need to be done away with? Should the church observe more silence and speak less? Should it at any rate carry out a quantitative reduction with regard to its speaking? The letter writer suggests this, but Bonhoeffer contradicts her. Had he not once written "that the problem is not that there is too much preaching, but that there is too much bad preaching" (see 3.5)? Not only does Dietrich Bonhoeffer have a biological father in Karl Bonhoeffer, but also a theological father in Karl Barth. Along with the influence of the man who had no desire to be the only one speaking every Sunday morning and therefore no desire to become a minister, he had also undergone the influence of a theology the heart of which lay in the preaching of the church as the center of the Sunday liturgy. Bonhoeffer considers the suggestion in the letter that it would be better to keep silent understandable, but at the same time a little "fashionable" and exaggerated. It is as if a preacher did not know what silence is! Bonhoeffer's answer is interesting enough to quote.

> We preachers experience it innumerable times in our pastoral work that a Bible passage read by a sick, poor, or lonely person is something totally different than when we would say it ourselves. For that reason we often enough keep silent, so as not to exercise our ministry as a spiritual routine. But we know that we sometimes must speak and often may not remain silent, even if we would prefer to do so. You should try to put yourself in our position, of having to deal "professionally" from early morning to late evening with the greatest words of the world, reading, studying, praying, teaching, baptizing, marrying, burying, and preaching. We cannot be thankful enough when people tell us what we do wrong, where we simply, perhaps with heart and soul, fall into speaking idle words. But above all we want to know how we could do it better. A desperate remedy, such as removing words like "cross," "sin," "grace," and so on from our vocabulary, will not help. In the first place a guillotine cannot be substituted for a cross, simply because Jesus died on a

cross. In the second place a word like "feeding trough" might for a moment be a good choice instead of "manger," but after three or four times it would be just as worn out. Of course there are words we should get rid of, especially our own favorite words that we have coined, but we have to speak words. Whether the "colloquial language of those with an average education" is the best, I do not know. It was at any rate not the language of Luther. I believe that we should not at all look for one style of speaking or another. We would then become too complacent. No one can alter the fact that Christianity is two thousand years old and has its own language. It is my conviction that the simple language of the Bible must remain. . . . But decisive is the depth out of which it arises and the surroundings in which it stands. Now, in conclusion, I have to say something "spiritual" to you. You certainly are familiar with the books of Bernanos. When ministers say something from them, then their words carry weight. That does not originate from some linguistic consideration or perception, but quite simply from the daily, personal encounter with the crucified Christ. It is a depth out of which a word must spring if it is to carry weight. One can also say that it depends on whether we judge ourselves daily by the image of the crucified Christ and let ourselves be called to conversion. Where a word, so to speak, comes with immediacy from the cross of Jesus Christ, where Christ is so present for us that it is he who speaks our word, only there can the terrible danger of spiritual small talk be banished. But who of us lives in such concentration? (*GS*, 3:42-43)

A number of elements from this letter are now familiar to us. I have already pointed to the preciousness of a word and the value of "prolonged silence." We have likewise a notion of what Bonhoeffer means by the condition of "depth" by which he wants to measure the weight of a word and by the emphasis on the "surroundings" that determine its meaning. The Word of God is apparently a *personal* word that is to be heard and spoken in a particular *situation*. For that reason a poor or sick person can at times speak it better than a pastor, who does better to keep silent, as Bonhoeffer the pastor has discerned. Even though he emphatically situates himself in the Reformation tradition and its concept of the church, that is, the church as "proclaimer of the Word of God," it is telling that he mentions pastoral care as a context for proclamation, a situation in which people speak face-to-face with each other, rather than in a public and anonymous sermon. Could not the attention for pastoral care as a context for proclamation also be related to the importance that was attributed to intimate, personal conversation in his upbringing? The situation of personal conversation is at any rate considered to be of essential importance for judging the way in which the church speaks of God (see 5.5).

There is, however, more that attracts our attention in the letter and that emerges when we compare it to the "Thoughts on the Day of Baptism," which Bonhoeffer would later write from prison. Four years separate the two texts and that is noticeable. In the baptismal sermon Bonhoeffer is much less certain about the church than here. His faith in ministry had been less tried in 1940 than in 1944. In the present letter the minister still stands in the center of the congregation and the church in the center of the town. Sometimes we *must* speak, Bonhoeffer says, even if at times we would prefer to keep silent. Our ministry demands that we not wordlessly teach, baptize, marry, bury, and so forth. The fearful question, whether all of that could not be better left undone because it has no meaning for people "as they are," had not yet loomed up in Bonhoeffer's horizon. That will occur later in prison (see 6.1).

At this point I wish to direct attention not so much to the shift between the two letters but rather to the recognizable continuity. Then it strikes me that in the letter now under consideration, four years prior to the baptismal sermon, Bonhoeffer does not localize the deficit primarily in the descriptive capacities of language, but rather in the pragmatic context in which the church speaks. The suggestion to find substitutes for certain words of the tradition can sometimes, in his judgment, provide a refreshing effect. If the opportunity arises, one should not let it pass by. But it is not the ultimate solution for the problem of a failing proclamation. The historical roots of Christianity do not need to be denied. The simple language of the Bible can remain.

It is above all the "depth out of which a word must spring if it is to carry weight" that is "decisive." The word "depth" would have remained vague had Bonhoeffer not immediately explained it. In the sentences that follow he points to the image of the crucified Christ that one should always keep in sight. Whoever does that, according to Bonhoeffer, hears the Word of God, so to speak, immediately from the cross. Christ is present in such a way that it is *he* who speaks *our* word directly.

These few sentences are enigmatic and compact. They arouse questions as to the clarity of their formulation, but we hear in them the vital heartbeat of Bonhoeffer's theology. It becomes clear that the "depth," out of which a responsible way of speaking about God arises, is to be found for Bonhoeffer not in a general condition of speech but in a specific, theological matrix. He makes a plea for an intensive practice of meditation with Christ as object, more specifically, "the image of the crucified Christ." It is a spiritual practice, in which one visualizes the image of Christ in the mind. This bringing to mind of Christ is a wordless event, appealing to our visual imagination. The spoken word of proclamation arises out of the intensity of that silent contemplation. The visual representation of Christ can be practiced with so much concentration that the experience of faith undergoes, as it were, a change as it reaches crescendo intensity. It is then as though, "so to speak," Christ is present in a manner that "it is he who speaks our word." In the mystical experience the roles seem to have been reversed. The believers have exchanged places with Christ. They no longer speak about Christ, but Christ speaks through them, directly. He, the object of faith, becomes the subject of the believer's speaking of God.

How inaccessible this mystical path seems to be, the ease with which pulpit orators seek to immunize their faith language from criticism by adorning it with a divine consecration, receives no support from Bonhoeffer. "The language of the Protestant church is no matter of secondary importance." Bonhoeffer binds the church's act of speaking to a number of general conditions, if it is to be effective. Like every word, a Christian word depends for its effectiveness on the credibility of the speaker ("depth") and the context or situation in which one speaks ("surroundings"). But all instances of speech, if they are not eventually to turn into idle chatter, must not only meet those conditions but also in turn be bound to a specific, ultimate measure, the Word of Christ. Proclamation is not in and of itself the Word of God, but it can become that Word. All speaking of God comes from below, but it does not have to stay there. The church's speaking is then no longer submitted to a linguistic but to a theological criterion. Responsible speaking of God has to be measured by the speaking of God in Christ. That requires, however, an intensive spiritual practice of listening.

4.2 "It Is God Who Must Speak on Sunday Morning" (The A Priori of Karl Barth)

But is it possible for God to speak a word? We encounter here the theological presupposition that Bonhoeffer derived from Karl Barth and that can be summarized in two words: *Deus dixit* (God has spoken). It implies as an irrelinquishable presupposition (1) that God speaks and (2) that God does so in Jesus Christ. Listening to God is thus prior to human speaking about God. Before we speak about God, God speaks about God. All of our speaking about God is a speaking after God's speaking and has to be measured by that speaking. The concentration of Christ and the intensive spirituality in which that a priori is cloaked is specific for Bonhoeffer. But that in human speaking about God the God who speaks can be heard is a presupposition that Bonhoeffer shared with Barth.

How strongly Barth influenced Bonhoeffer is still a matter of discussion in interpretations of Bonhoeffer.[1] The fact remains that it was incisive. When in 1931 Bonhoeffer had experienced Barth in Bonn and was

---

1. That the liberal theologian Adolf von Harnack left his mark on the thought of Bonhoeffer becomes more and more clear. Besides chap. 3, n.16 above, see R. Staats, "Adolf von Harnack im Leben Dietrich Bonhoeffers" (Adolph von Harnack in the life of Dietrich Bonhoeffer), *Theologische Zeitschrift* 37/2 (1981) 94-121. Staats's hypothesis that von Harnack had determinant influence on Bonhoeffer's theology from 1924 on has been contested by H. E. Tödt, "Dietrich Bonhoeffer's ökumenische Friedensethik" (Dietrich Bonhoeffer's ecumenical ethic of peace), in *Frieden — das unumgängliche Wagnis* (Peace — the inescapable venture), Internationales Bonhoeffer Forum 5 (Munich: Chr. Kaiser, 1982), 114, who in Bonhoeffer's early writings (especially from Barcelona in 1928; cf. *GS*, 5:147ff., 422) already finds traces of dialectical theology. A discussion like this can in my opinion not be decided as long as it is carried on in terms of more or less. Barth is emphatically present in Bonhoeffer's theology from 1925 on, a fact that can be illustrated with the help of recently published seminar papers (*DBW*, 9, especially the paper on historic and pneumatic interpretation of Scripture from 1925, 205-323). For a detailed analysis of the Barth-Bonhoeffer relationship see Charles Marsh, *Reclaiming Dietrich Bonhoeffer: The Promise of His Theology* (New York/Oxford: Oxford University Press, 1994), 7-33.

For Bonhoeffer's own description of his theological mixed lineage ("Bastard-Herkunft"), see *GS*, 1:19 (1931). Cf. also his characterization of himself as "one who, although a 'modern' [= dialectical] theologian, is aware of the debt he owes to liberal theology" (*LPP*, 378). His independence with respect to Barth appears not only in his letters from prison but also in his comment when he is passed over for a contribution to a volume on the occasion of Barth's fiftieth birthday. It is not such a disaster after all, he says, because "I do not want to be branded as a Barthian, for I'm not one" (quoted in Zimmermann and Smith, *I Knew Dietrich Bonhoeffer*, 66). That Barth's theology affected him more than he let be known we can read in a letter to Barth from 1936 (*TF*, 430) written after a period without contact with each other. "The whole period was basically a constant, silent controversy with you, and so I had to keep silent for a while." Again the silence of Bonhoeffer proves to be very telling.

deeply impressed by the man and his lectures, he admitted in a letter to Erwin Sutz: "I don't think that I have ever regretted anything that I have failed to do in my theological past as much as the fact that I did not come here earlier" (*TF*, 383). Shortly before, in an address in New York on "The Theology of Crisis and Its Attitude Toward Philosophy and Science," he had already left the impression on his American audience that he was a passionate defender of Barth's position (*GS*, 3:110-26). Much earlier he had acquainted himself with Barth's writings. Since he had read Barth's volume of articles *The Word of God and the Word of Man* in 1925, Bonhoeffer's thought was decisively affected by the critical turn that Barth had taken in theology. In a paper written as a student in 1925 Bonhoeffer reproduced Barth's thought without hesitation, stating that when God speaks in the Bible, human beings cannot hear it, but only God. "Like can only be known by like, God by God." How can one then ever speak of God? Bonhoeffer's solution is that of Barth, and ultimately the same as we encountered in the "letter to an unknown woman," even if somewhat more abstractly formulated. "The object of knowledge creates in the subject organs for knowing in the act of knowledge itself" (*DBW*, 9:312). Only God can make God audible and understandable. Bonhoeffer would henceforth remain a critical and independent, but nevertheless resolute, ally of Barth's theology.[2]

Barth considered his project to be an answer to nineteenth-century liberal theology, which reduced God to an extension of human thought and action, to the detriment of the godliness of God. One spoke enthusiastically about God, but what, Barth asks, did one describe that was more and different than oneself and one's own exalted religious and moral feelings? In the lectures "History of the Systematic Theology in the Twentieth Century" that Bonhoeffer delivered at the University of Berlin from 1931 to 1933 (*GS*, 5:181-227; *DBW*, 11:139-213), he outlines the decisive "turn" that Barth had taken by breaking with that theological tradition. At the end Bonhoeffer asks a few critical questions, such as how things should then further proceed, but essentially he speaks without serious reservations, so that one is at times uncertain who is speaking, Barth or Bonhoeffer.

Barth wanted to speak again God's truth. In his lectures on the history of theology Bonhoeffer identified that as Barth's motivation.[3] Of

---

2. For this characterization, see the afterword to *CF*, 152.

course his theology bears the mark of the cultural context of World War I, but Barth must first of all be seen as a theologian, not as a philosopher of culture. "Barth does not come out of the trenches, but out of a Swiss village pulpit." "The turn is not enacted as something generally historical, but within theology. He really wants again to 'speak correctly of God'" (*GS*, 5:216-17; *DBW*, 11:196). For Bonhoeffer the starting point for Barth's "theology of crisis" lies not in the trenches but in the pulpit.

> That is where "God's Word" has to be said, that is where God is to speak. And yet I speak, a human being. I have to speak, and nevertheless it is not I, but God. I must recognize that I am not capable of it. I can do nothing else than *speak* about God, in the expectation that God will make of my speaking something that it can never be of itself, God's own Word. Barth's theology has its starting point in this problematic of preaching and the concern for it. . . . It must be God who speaks at 10 o'clock on Sunday morning. Everything depends on that event. On the other hand it is of subordinate importance whether the sermon is exalted or simple, excitingly interesting or boring. The words of the preacher are like spokes in a wheel. The hole in the middle remains empty, that is, God sees to it that the hole is filled and that the spokes fulfill their function. (*GS*, 5:216-17; *DBW*, 11:196; see 1.2 above)

It is Barth's intention again to create space for God to act freely in theology. "God is the coming one. That is God's transcendence. One can only 'have' God if one expects God. At the start of theology one should speak about the Word of God rather than about religion." Religion is and remains the work of human beings, whereas speaking about the Word of God presupposes that it is God who must say that God is the absolute beginning. "Only where God alone speaks do we know something about God. No subsequently postulated concept of revelation makes God speak. Only through the revelation that occurs of its own accord can we know

3. With respect to Barth Bonhoeffer refers especially to his *Römerbrief* (1922) (*The Epistle to the Romans*, trans. Edwyn C. Hoskyns [Oxford: Oxford University Press, 1968]); *Christliche Dogmatik* (1927) (*The Göttingen Dogmatics: Instructions in the Christian Religion*, vol. 1, ed. Hannelotte Reiffen, trans. G. W. Bromiley [Grand Rapids: Eerdmans, 1991]); *Kirchliche Dogmatik*, I/1 (1932) (*Church Dogmatics*, I/1, trans. G. T. Thompson [Edinburgh: T. & T. Clark, 1936; 2d ed. trans. G. W. Bromiley, ed. Bromiley and T. F. Torrance, 1975]). See the editorial references in *DBW*, 11.

God as the beginning that cannot be further grounded and that is itself the ground of all things" (*GS,* 5:219; *DBW,* 11:199).

How then can one ever speak about God if there exists such a diastasis between God and human beings? How can God's Word ever be spoken by human lips? How can the "Word in the words" ever be heard? That can occur only through a "miracle," according to the young Barth in his "theology of crisis." The later Barth sought possibilities for not only setting negative limits but for speaking positively of the God who speaks. In the *Church Dogmatics,* which Barth began writing in 1932, he modified his diastatic viewpoint on God's speaking. Originally he presented a doctrine of the three "forms" of the Word of God, in which preaching as the *proclaimed* Word is subordinate to the Bible (the *written* Word of God), which in turn witnesses to the revelation of God in the history of Israel and in the person of Jesus Christ (the *revealed* Word of God). Later, in his doctrine of reconciliation (*Church Dogmatics,* IV/1ff.), Barth reserved the name "Word of God" more exclusively for Jesus Christ. He alone is the Word of God. Bible and preaching witness to the Word of God. They are no longer paradoxically identified with the Word but form an analogy to it.[4]

When Bonhoeffer in his outline from 1931 did not directly interpret the human possibility (or impossibility) of speaking about God as a logical paradox, but pointed to the person of Jesus Christ as the intelligible Word of God, then one observes that he has already placed his own accent on the basis of his own theological suppositions. One does not yet find the same christological accent in Barth as when Bonhoeffer states that "God's revelation occurs in the person of Christ and it does so in an intelligible manner. That word, Christ, is really God in total freedom, and at the same time shrouded in the cloak of history, humanity. To be sure God is something totally different from a human being, but when God speaks, it is in a shrouded, that is, in a human manner. . . . We would know nothing of God if he did not come in that way. That God comes in that way is a mystery. . . . The Word of God is the eminent petitio principii [necessity of evidence]. Deus dixit [God has spoken], that is to be accepted as the beginning of all theological thinking" (*GS,* 5:219; *DBW,* 11:199).

4. See on this development A. Grözinger, *Die Sprache des Menschen: Ein Handbuch; Grundwissen für Theologinnen und Theologen* (Human language: A manual; basic knowledge for theologians) (Munich: Chr. Kaiser, 1991), 223ff.

Bonhoeffer was aware that, while such a theological starting point can prove fruitful for the church, it is philosophically problematic. Can theology still be a science if it begins with such a priori presuppositions? Bonhoeffer openly recognized that such a theology that makes God the subject of theology before becoming its object is quite vulnerable. But the gain from that beginning (and one notices that Bonhoeffer wants to place all the emphasis on that) is much greater than the loss. Theology reopens its senses for the godliness of God in divine activity. It does not enclose God in its speaking, but first listens with receptivity before daring to speak about God. "The object of theology is only the *Logos Theou* [Word of God], the self-grounded activity of God. Behind that beginning we cannot pry" (*GS*, 5:219; *DBW*, 11:199).

4.3 The Given Word (The Concentration on Christology)

As already indicated, Bonhoeffer also had objections to Barth's theology. But they do not weigh up against the fundamental agreement that he felt. Barth taught him to be a theologian, one who speaks of God, rather than the scholar of religion that the liberal tradition would have made of him. He learned to become a preacher, who does more than arouse religious sentiments like the preachers in his youth, a preacher in whose words God speaks. The theologian of the Word gave theology back to the church and placed it again at the service of proclamation. So, too, the dialectical theology gave the academic scholar Bonhoeffer to the church.

Bonhoeffer had already expressed his critique of Barth in his dissertations. The major one had to do with the actualism and individualism of Barth's epistemology and the abstract arbitrariness that followed for ethics. How can one ever proclaim God's command concretely if a human word can only become a divine word by means of a miracle? The Lutheran Bonhoeffer sought in the second instance to conceive of God and humanity as being much closer to each other than the Reformed Church theologian Barth. Whereas the latter anchored knowledge of God in the knowing individual, Bonhoeffer tied it to the community of the church. Even before Barth began publishing his *Church Dogmatics*, Bonhoeffer had written an ecclesiological study (*Sanctorum Communio* [The Communion of Saints], 1927) in which the church was understood not only as an object of theology but also as its presupposition.

I will not now go into the further differences between Barth and Bonhoeffer. I only note that Bonhoeffer's critique was not prompted by other philosophical or theological presuppositions, but precisely by his even greater emphasis on the central element of Christian tradition that both of their theologies took as a starting point and that made them allies more than that it divided them, namely, the presupposition that God has spoken God's Word in Jesus Christ. Whereas Barth initially placed all emphasis on the act of God's sovereign freedom in that speaking, Bonhoeffer accentuated that which was spoken. God has *given* God's Word, he emphasized in *Act and Being* (1931). God's freedom consists of the fact that God has freely bound the divine being to human beings. That concrete fact must put an end to any actualism, by which God, following an eventual but fully contingent speaking, withdraws into an unassailable and inaccessible *aseitas*. "God is free not from human beings but for them. Christ is the word of God's freedom" (*AB*, 90-91). In the proclaimed Christ, according to Bonhoeffer in the same *Act and Being*, God is tangible, can be "had" in God's Word in the church. Revelation can be held onto there.

That starting point in Christology is a structural element in all of Bonhoeffer's theology. It becomes even more emphatic the more his theology is deepened and developed. By that I do not mean to say that one comes across more and more explicit christological reflections in his writings, but that one encounters an ever more intensive triangular relation between biographical experience, theological reflection, and Christ-centered piety. The question "Who is Christ for us today?" is the starting point for Bonhoeffer's reflections from prison on a nonreligious interpretation of Christian faith and underlies all of his theology. His theology is pervaded with Christocentrism, even if it is not continually explicit Christology. That Christocentrism is in turn fed by a faith experience, which can best be called a form of Christ mysticism, provided that one does not take it to be a sort of escapism.[5]

That piety is encountered only sporadically in Bonhoeffer's early writings. Even if Christ is more than a code word there, Bonhoeffer's early Christology appears bloodless and pale. In vain does one look for a statement such as in the letters: "If we are to learn what God promises, and what God fulfills, we must persevere in quiet meditation on the life, say-

---

5. Cf. Abromeit, *Das Geheimnis Christi*, 16ff.

DEUS DIXIT | 75

ings, deeds, sufferings, and the death of Jesus" (*LPP*, 391; August 21, 1944). "Christ as the Word of God" seems at times an image that does not go beyond its strategic function. But for Bonhoeffer Christ becomes gradually more than a theological construct and grows to be a living reality, the sustaining ground for his theological vocation. In the metaphor "Christ as the Word of God," Bonhoeffer encounters the speaking God, who calls him to follow.[6]

The religious experience underlying that deepening, in reference to which Bethge speaks of a "transition from theologian to Christian," is not available for empirical scrutiny. Bonhoeffer never revealed anything on how, where, or when his "conversion" occurred.[7] He considered that to be a personal, intimate matter, on which one should keep silent. In 1936 he did write to Elisabeth Zinn, the woman who once almost became his spouse, that "something happened, something has changed and transformed my life to the present day." He admits to her that he is no longer the ambitious theologian of a few years before. He explains, "For the first time I discovered the Bible. . . . I had often preached, I had seen a great deal of the church, and talked and preached about it — but I had not yet become a Christian" (*GS*, 6:367-68).[8] However one interprets that experience, it is a fact that one cannot comprehend Bonhoeffer's theology apart from it. The commitment and spirituality that pervade Bonhoeffer's theology hang loose up in the air of abstraction if one does not ascertain, as Ebeling tersely declared in 1955, that "the simple fact is: Jesus Christ has met him, he knows himself called and claimed by Jesus Christ."[9]

6. Cf. Bethge, *Dietrich Bonhoeffer*, 378, on the Christology of *The Cost of Discipleship*, which continues in the line of the academic lectures of 1933. "Here we may see how, by interpreting belief in Christ as discipleship, he succeeds in putting new life into the sawdust puppet of academic Christology."

7. It is probably better to speak with J. Glentøj of a growing sense of calling. Bonhoeffer often compared his position and role with that of prophets like Moses, Jonah, and Jeremiah ("Dietrich Bonhoeffers Weg vom Pazifismus zum politischen Widerstand" (Dietrich Bonhoeffer's way from pacifism to political resistance), in R. Mayer and P. Zimmerling, *Dietrich Bonhoeffer heute* (Dietrich Bonhoeffer today) (Giessen/Basel: Brunnen, 1992), 41-57.

8. Cf. Bethge, *Dietrich Bonhoeffer*, 154.

9. Ebeling, "The 'Non-religious Interpretation of Biblical Concepts,'" 109.

4.4 Christ as Idea and as Address

That observation is of decisive importance for Bonhoeffer's views on speaking about God. The Word of God was for him not only a theological concept but also a living reality. In the person of Jesus Christ he encountered a God who spoke to him personally.

His lectures on Christology in 1933, despite their academic rigor, reflect that encounter. Even the arrangement of his material is surprisingly revealing. The first main section is titled "The present Christ — the *pro me*"; Bonhoeffer does not treat the historical Christ until the second section. The reality of the living Christ is his primary concern. He interprets Christ theologically with the help of the concept of personhood, which he could borrow from contemporary philosophy. But his own religious-humanistic upbringing also had a say here (see 3.4). Christ is for him the preeminent person, who (and that is for Bonhoeffer characteristic of what personal is) avoids the grasping by which people attempt conceptually to get a grip on each other and reduce each other to controllable property. Christ is completely transcendent. Bonhoeffer can express the same in the language of faith of Christian tradition, namely, that in Jesus Christ God is present. That is also the a priori that he in the line of Barth wants to take as a starting point for theology. "This one God-human is the starting point for Christology" (*CC*, 45).

But where is Christ truly present for us, if he is more than a historical Jesus figure? If he is by definition beyond human conception, how can one ever say anything meaningful about him? Bonhoeffer answers that Christ is present for us in the human word of proclamation. "The presence of the already given God-human Jesus is concealed for us, and exists in the *scandalon* form of proclamation. . . . The proclaimed Christ is the real Christ" (*CC*, 45). But is the expression "Christ present in human words" not like making a virtue of religious necessity, that is, admitting the inability to speak of God? No, answers Bonhoeffer, for it is only to follow on the way that God has gone before. In Christ God has let the deity be tailored to human size. God has, says the Bible, been humbled and entered into human reality. Human reality, according to Bonhoeffer, contains three aspects, from the points of view of the speaking, the bodily, or the social human being. In that threefold framework of our reality the figure of Christ is present, as language (word), as matter (sacrament), and as society (community).

It is a bold construction. My concern here is not whether it is tenable. I only observe the theological primacy that Bonhoeffer attributes to "Christ as Word." The section with that title begins as follows. "Christ the Word is truth. There is no truth apart from the Word and by the Word. Spirit is originally word and language, not power, feeling or act. 'In the beginning was the Word . . . and all things were made through the Word' (John 1:1, 3). Only as Word is the Spirit also power and act. God's Word creates and destroys. 'The Word of God is . . . sharper than any two-edged sword, piercing to the division' (Hebrews 4:12). God's Word carries the destroying lightning and the life-giving rain. As Word, it destroys and creates the truth" (*CC*, 49).

Like the Bible, Bonhoeffer binds God to words. Language is the preferential means of God. It is a fictitious proposition (for who has ever literally heard God speak?) that is quite significant in its consequences. It makes of God a very humanlike God, with whom one can communicate. God is not a dumb power that overwhelms, nor a substance that one encounters, but a Word that appeals to human beings. It could have been otherwise. "It is playing games to ask whether God is able to reveal God in any other way than through the Word. Of course God has the freedom to reveal God in other ways than we know. But God *has* revealed divinity in the Word. God has been bound to the Word that God might speak to humankind. God does not alter this Word" (*CC*, 49; translation slightly altered).

In Bonhoeffer's interpretation of the biblical story of creation, *Creation and Fall*, on which he had just previously given lectures (1932-33), he also made an emphatic case for the word character of the Christian concept of God. Bonhoeffer echoes Genesis when he states that God creates the world by his Word and does not coincide with it as substance (*CF*, 40-44). Is God's Word then reduced to a human word from the beginning? No, in Bonhoeffer's judgment, because then there would not have been a created world at all. He attributes to the original Word of God a performative power, an effect that our words severely lack (see 2.2). The Word of God is an active word *(Tatwort)* that does what it says. It does not function as a symbol, meaning, or idea of something, but it makes that which is named present: "God's word *is* already the work" (*CF*, 42).[10] What

---

10. Cf. *CF*, 42 nn. 9 and 10: "The word is itself the deed," with reference to Ps. 33:9: "as God commands, so it stands forth."

for us hopelessly falls apart is for God inseparably bound, the indicative and the imperative, the command and the event. We, as Bonhoeffer observes in his lectures on Christology, have fallen from the unity of that "action-word" (Hebrew *dabar*). "The fallen creation is no longer the creation of the first creative word" (*CC*, 53). The Word of God interprets itself unambiguously. The identity of a word and the thing referred to has given way in our world to ambiguity. The continuity between word and reality has been broken. The first language was ruined (*CC*, 31). Human beings stand in the midst of a mute, silenced world and hear only themselves, not God, speaking in things (*CF*, 142). With the Bible (cf. the question "Where are you?" in Gen. 3:9) Bonhoeffer locates the cause of the absence of the word, the silence of God, in ourselves. It is human beings who have withdrawn from being addressed by God (*CF*, 108).[11] It is a result of sin that we no longer hear the living God who directs God's Word to us.

Is nothing left than to be silent? At this point Bonhoeffer brings in his theological a priori: Christ as the Word of God that speaks again to human beings in the midst of their silent world. It is a Word of God that has taken on the form of a human word. In its paradoxical weakness it shows its strength. Again Bonhoeffer does not mean a symbol or sign by the "word" character of Christ. That also would bring that Word down into human reach. Symbols and signs are our products, our creation. Bonhoeffer characterizes the divine Word as that which was from the beginning, namely, address. In this context he sharply contrasts word as idea and word as address. Christ is "the Word in the form of living address to men, but the word of men is word in the form of the idea. Address and idea are the basic structures of the word. But they exclude each other" (*CC*, 50).

Bonhoeffer opposes here the philosophical tradition in which he as a liberal theologian was brought up, that of idealism. Now it has become for him a model for sinful thinking. He notes that human thinking is dominated by the word as idea. Whoever describes Christ as the Word of God in terms of an "idea" makes of him a timeless, eternal truth, available and accessible for everyone anywhere at any time. But Bonhoeffer objects to this abstract reductionism:

11. Cf. *GS*, 5:293 ("Gibt es eine christliche Ethik?" [Does a Christian ethics exist?] [1932]): "Creation remains mute, if Christ does not speak. . . . The muteness of creation is an expression of its depravity."

The Word as address stands in contrast to this. While it is possible for the Word as idea to remain by itself, as address it is only possible between two. Address requires response and responsibility. It is not timeless but happens in history. It does not rest and is not accessible to anyone at any time. It happens only when the address is made. The word lies wholly and freely at the disposal of the one who speaks. Thus it is unique and every time new.[12] Its character as address requires the community. The character of truth in this addressing word is such that it seeks community, in order to face it with the truth. Truth is not something in itself, which rests for itself, but something that happens between two. Truth happens only in community. It is here for the first time that the concept of the Word acquires its full significance. (*CC*, 50)

Just as we discern in his protest against "idea" a protest against idealism, we can observe in his concept of truth his proximity to existential and dialectical philosophy. Truth is not the correspondence between a thing and an idea, but is personal. However indebted Bonhoeffer is to philosophy, his intention is not philosophical but theological. He wishes to understand Christ, the Word of God, as a personal address that asks a human being to answer, that calls one to responsibility before one can answer. "Christ becomes the address of forgiveness and command" (*CC*, 51).

By presenting Christ as an active and community-seeking Word of God, Bonhoeffer sees the chasm between human words and the Word of God bridged. Because God speaks in human language, one can speak humanly of God. But does God's conformity to human words mean that he coincides with them and becomes a victim of sin, that is, the division between word and effect, thinking and doing? No, Christ remains God's efficacious, reality-creating Word, and as such he takes form in our midst. The Christ-Word is as an address for God's sake present and active among us in the proclamation of the *Word*, and consequently, also as a form of God's Word, as *sacrament* and as *community* (see above).

12. On the same contrast between idea and the Word of God, cf. *CD*, 166: "An ideology requires fanatics . . . it is certainly a potent force. But the Word of God in its weakness takes the risk of meeting the scorn of men and being rejected." Cf. ibid., 206n.1: "The direct testimony of the Scriptures is frequently confounded with ontological propositions. This error is the essence of fanaticism in all its forms. . . . The assertion that Jesus Christ is risen and present, is, when taken strictly as a testimony given in the Scriptures, true only as a word of the Scriptures. This word is the object of our faith. There is no other conceivable way of approach to this truth except through this word."

Bonhoeffer does not narrow the Word of God to the sermon. It is more than a word from the pulpit. It is also sacrament and church, matter and social community (see below and 4.3). But it is certainly also spoken language. "Christ is not only present *in* the Word of the Church, but also *as* Word of the Church, that means the spoken Word of preaching. . . . Christ's presence is his existence as proclamation. The whole Christ is present in preaching, humiliated and exalted. . . . If that were not so, preaching could not have that prominent place which the Reformation insisted upon. This place belongs to the simplest sermon. The sermon is both the riches and the poverty of the Church. It is the form of the present Christ to which we are bound and to which we must hold. If the complete Christ is not in the preaching, then the Church is broken" (*CC*, 51-52).

4.5 The Inexpressible

With regard to the relation between human word and divine Word in preaching, Bonhoeffer states in his lectures on Christology that one should not define them in terms of an exclusive identity. One should conceive of their relationship analogously to the divine and human Christ. Just as God has been humbled by freely binding the divine reality to the human condition in Christ, God does the same with regard to preaching. "The human word of preaching is the Word of God, because God has freely bound the deity and is bound to the word of human beings. Luther wrote, 'To this man you point and say: there is God.' We would alter it slightly: 'To this human word you should point and say: that is the Word of God.' . . . So Christ is present in the Church as spoken Word, not as music nor as art. Present as the spoken Word of judgement and forgiveness. Two things have to be said here with equal emphasis: I could not preach if I did not know that I spoke *the Word of God* — and: I could not preach did I not know that *I* cannot say the Word of God. What is impossible for human beings and what God promises are the same" (*CC*, 52; translation slightly altered).

The homiletic theory that Bonhoeffer develops here, and that will concern us more in the following chapter, is similar to that of the early Barth. Both begin from a structural deficit of human words and a gracious profusion of the divine Word. But whereas according to the young Reformed Church theologian Barth the diastasis between God's Word and a human word cannot be sufficiently emphasized (for according to the Calvinist adage, "finitum non capax infinitum," i.e., that which is finite cannot comprehend that which is infinite), the Lutheran Bonhoeffer brings them very close together on account of the incarnation (to be sure, only by God's initiative).

I cannot deal with Bonhoeffer's homiletics at greater length except to emphasize again that for him proclamation did not coincide with the sermon. God does not speak only from the pulpit. God also speaks, as we heard in Bonhoeffer's lectures on Christology, in the sacrament and as community. Bonhoeffer points to both sacrament and community as Word. On sacrament he states: "The sacrament is Word of God, because it is proclamation of the Gospel. It is not a mystery or mute symbolic action, but its action is consecrated and interpreted by the Word. . . . The Word in the sacrament is embodied Word" (CC, 52-53). "Is there a Christ of the sacrament and a Christ of preaching? Is the one who is present as sacrament different from the one who is present in the Word? No! He is the one judging and forgiving Christ, who is the Word, in both. . . . He is the Word of God which has become bread and wine" (CC, 57). With regard to community Bonhoeffer continues. "What does it mean that Christ as *Word* is also community? It means that the Logos of God has existence in space and time in and as the community. Christ the Word is spiritually and physically present. . . . The Word is *in* the community in so far as the community is a recipient of revelation. But the Word is also itself community, in so far as the community itself is revelation and the Word wishes to have the form of a created body" (CC, 58-59; translation slightly altered).[13]

I cannot here pursue the line of this doctrine of the sacrament and of ecclesiology further. I can, nevertheless, conclude that Bonhoeffer apparently attributes the same effective power to the Word of God in the church as he does to the creative Word of God in the beginning. When the Word of God is spoken, it creates its own reality. The gap between a word and a thing is overcome. The name becomes the matter itself. The word becomes embodied. Time and space become social community. The Logos is a "powerful Word of the Creator" (CC, 58). The emphasis on the concreteness of the Word of God assures that, whatever accent the proclamation of the Word receives from the Lutheran Bonhoeffer, the proclamation of the

13. Cf. the mutual presupposition of Word and community (= church) in CS, 161: "The church makes the Word just as the Word makes the church."

gospel never becomes mere wordiness.[14] On the contrary, if one conceives of the profusion of the divine Word so materially as Bonhoeffer does, one will be more likely to suffer from a church whose proclamation gets bogged down in empty words.

The Word of God is for Bonhoeffer of a quality that causes human words to turn pale. It is God's Word, and before we speak about it, we have to realize in what relation we stand to it. The opening of the lectures on Christology invites us to do so. The only adequate posture toward the Word of God is, so we hear, silence. This silence, as we have seen, stands in the context of a God who speaks, not a silent God. The silence to which Bonhoeffer calls us is a silence out of respect for the excess of the word, not a silence that arises from the Word withdrawing itself, an echo of a mute universe.

> Teaching about Christ begins in silence. "Be still, for that is the absolute," writes Kierkegaard. This has nothing to do with silence of the mystics, who in their dumbness chatter away secretly in their soul by themselves. The silence of the Church is silence before the Word. In so far as the Church proclaims the Word, it falls down silently in truth before the inexpressible. "In silence I worship the unutterable" (Cyril of Alexandria). The spoken Word is the inexpressible: this unutterable is the Word. "It must become spoken, it is the great battle cry" (Luther). Although it is cried out by the Church in the world, it remains the inexpressible. To speak of Christ means to keep silent; to be silent about Christ means to speak. When the Church speaks rightly out of a proper silence, then Christ is proclaimed. . . . Here to speak of Christ will be thus to speak in the silent places of the Church. In the humble silence of the worshipping congregation we concern ourselves with christology. To pray is to be silent and at the same time to cry out, before God and in the presence of God's Word. It is for the study of Christ, that is, God's Word, that we have gathered together as a congregation. (*CC*, 27)

Bonhoeffer could hardly have more strongly described the profusion of the divine Word and the limits of a human word. He remained within the focus of the Reformation on the proclamation of the Word, but he was

---

14. Cf. *WP*, 140 (lectures on homiletics, 1935): "The sermon is concrete only when God's word is really in it. God alone is the *concretissimum*." Cf. in this context the comment by Zimmermann, *Bruder Bonhoeffer*, 84: "Bonhoeffer had a very substantive conception of the power of the word."

aware, as none other, of the fact that the extremes of silence and screaming touch each other in the face of the God who speaks. Bonhoeffer developed his theological theory of church proclamation as a Lutheran, who in the line of Barth had learned that God wants to speak for God in the church. On the one hand, it was the wariness of great words that Bonhoeffer learned at home that prevented him from weakening his voice. On the other hand, it was the encounter of faith with the living Christ that evoked a religious awe and humility, and that prevented Bonhoeffer from reducing Christ to a concept.

In a Christmas meditation from 1940, he says of the Christ-child: "Only stammeringly can one utter his name, can one seek to describe what the name entails. The words pile up and tumble over each other, while seeking to express who this child is" (GS, 4:573). It seems that more words are needed than are available. But a little further in the same text it becomes apparent that the excess of words arises out of their lack of expressiveness. "We attempt to grasp in concepts what lies contained in the one name of Jesus. The words are, in fact, nothing else than a wordless silence in adoration of the inexpressible, of the presence of God in the form of a human child" (GS, 4:575).[15]

Between the God who speaks and the human being who hears there is an asymmetry, which a human being must not seek to manage of one's own accord. Christ is for us a strange Word coming from outside, *extra nos*, says Bonhoeffer in keeping with Luther (*E*, 188). It does not come out of us and cannot be incorporated by us. Why did God speak that Word? Why did he not observe an ultimate silence? We encounter here a mystery, which becomes greater the more we know about it. Or to put it differently, it fills us with more silence the more we say about it.[16] Three years before

15. Cf. the passage in *LPP*, 157, already quoted in chapter 2: "It is only when one knows the unutterability of the name of God that one can utter the name of Jesus Christ."

16. In a Christmas sermon from 1939 we hear, "'God revealed in the flesh,' the God-human Jesus Christ, that is the holy mystery that theology is endowed to protect and preserve. What a misunderstanding that the task of theology is to solve the enigma of God's mystery, to bring it down to the flat wisdom of human experience and reason, devoid of all mystery! Whereas this is its only office, to preserve God's miracle as a miracle, to comprehend, defend, and glorify God's mystery as mystery" (*GS*, 3:382). For the significance of the category of mystery (*Geheimnis*), see especially Feil, *Theology of Dietrich Bonhoeffer*, 5ff. There one finds more references to Bonhoeffer's writings. For a general reevaluation of the concept in systematic theology, see Jüngel, *God as the Mystery*, 246-61.

Bonhoeffer recognized in the baptismal sermon how much difficulty the church has in speaking of God, we find similar words in another letter written to a student from Finkenwalde who had been sent to the front lines after the seminary had been closed. Those words make clear that the speechlessness does not arise out of a despair of faith or out of theological weakness, but out of an awareness of the mystery of God. "There are times when all of reality is puzzling to us and so suppressive that each word seems to injure the mystery. Everything that we know to say about our faith seems so dull and empty in the face of the reality with which we are confronted and behind which we believe there is an inexpressible mystery. For you there it will not be much different than for us here at home. Everything we utter is blown away in a moment of time. Everything we formulate no longer fits reality. It can only be something quite authentic when one word, namely, Jesus Christ, does not fall away for us. That name remains a word, the Word, around which all of our words keep circling. In that word alone lies clarity and power" (*GS*, 2:577; August 15, 1941).[17]

The spoken word must yield to the mystery of Christ, which transcends the limits of words. I already mentioned the silence referred to in the lectures on Christology, but I conclude here by again recalling the passage from Bonhoeffer's letter to an unknown woman on the image of Christ (4.1), an image that believers are continually to envision so that Christ might become present to them. The *Cost of Discipleship* concludes with an entire chapter bearing the title "The Image of Christ." The Word of God sounds in that book a call to a radical following of Christ. It is a command that not only invokes hearing but issues an appeal for total obedience. Again Bonhoeffer emphasizes the performative power of the proclamation of the gospel. The Word is only heard if it has a life-changing influence. At the conclusion of the book Bonhoeffer asks what the ultimate purpose of discipleship is. "Those who follow Christ are destined to bear his image, and to be the brethren of the firstborn Son of God. Their goal is to become 'as Christ.' Christ's followers always have his image before their eyes, and in its light all other images are screened from their sight. It penetrates into the depths of their being, fills them, and makes them more and more like their Master. . . . No follower of Jesus can contemplate his image

---

17. Bonhoeffer subscribed to Chalcedon (451) but interpreted its negative and paradoxical formula (unconfusedly, unchangeably, indivisibly, inseparably) as a statement that bursts all forms of thought (*CC*, 88).

in a spirit of cold detachment. That image has the power to transform our lives" (*CD*, 269). It is a remarkable conclusion to a book that is almost completely devoted to hearing the call of Christ. But the "image of Christ" is for Bonhoeffer apparently nothing else than what he elsewhere calls the mystery of the Word of God, namely, the *transforming presence of God's salvation*. Just as silence before Christ is a manner of speaking for Bonhoeffer, so also does the image speak a language that can be called to help when the profusion of the Word of God is beyond the reach of human words.[18]

18. Cf. also *CD*, 126; *E*, 61; *CF*, 81; *LT*, 85-86. For more on the image of Christ in Bonhoeffer's writings, see Wendel, *Studien*, 152, 214.

5 A Red Apple, a Glass of Cool Water

Proclamation in the Church

S harp insight into the limits of human words combined with high expectations of the profusion of the Word of God constitutes Bonhoeffer's starting point for reflection on and an evaluation of proclamation in the church. The Word of God was dynamic for him, an explosive,
creative power as in the beginning. At the same time he considered human
words to be just as weak and sinful as the human beings from whose
mouth they come forth. Nevertheless in the timely proclamation of the
gospel in the church he bound the former to the latter. In *The Cost of Discipleship* he quotes the commission of Jesus: "As you go, proclaim the good
news, 'The kingdom of heaven has come near.' Cure the sick, raise the
dead, cast out demons. You received without payment, give without payment" (Matt. 10:7-8). Bonhoeffer considered the commission to apply directly to the church. Just as Jesus himself traveled throughout the land
through his twelve apostles, so does the church make Christ present today.
"The message becomes an event, and the event confirms the message. . . .
The proclamation of the apostles is the Word of the Almighty God, and,
therefore, it is an act, an event, a miracle. . . . The sovereign grace with
which they are equipped is the creative and redemptive Word of God"
(*CD*, 185).[1]

The original Word of God, which as command and promise called
the world into being, is inaccessible for us. The "first language" was ruined

1. Cf. *CD*, 182: "It is not a word or a doctrine they [the apostles] receive, but effective power."

in the fall, according to Bonhoeffer in his lectures on Christology (*CC*, 31). But in the lectures on homiletics that he held in 1935-1939 at Finkenwalde, he supports the position that, thanks to Christ, the original divine Word with all its "power" is again audible in Christian proclamation. It sounds exalted when he says, "The word of proclamation is not one species of the genus 'word,' but rather it is just the opposite: all of our words are species of the one, original Word of God which both creates and sustains the world. The world and all of its words exist for the sake of the proclaimed Word. For the sake of the proclaimed word the world exists with all of its words. In the sermon the foundation for a new world is laid. Here the original word becomes audible. There is no evading or getting away from the spoken word of the sermon" (*WP*, 130). Bonhoeffer places such extremely high expectations on preaching that it must have made an overstrained impression on his students. But their teacher, much to his own surprise if we can believe Bethge, appears quite resolute in his judgment. "This is the way we must learn to look at the sermon again" (*WP*, 130).[2] That the Word of God's grace had become "a sleeping pill" for "countless Christians" (*SC*, 31) was unbearable for him.

5.1 The Poverty of the Word

I have already emphasized that Bonhoeffer understood proclamation of the Word of God to entail more than the Sunday sermon from the pulpit. Now I must also emphasize that at least in his lectures on Christology he counted sacrament and the social community of the congregation as "forms of the Word." The Word spoken in Christ is, as *Logos Theou*, the expression of God's activity. It wants to become flesh and blood, time and space, and social community in this world. Nevertheless, in the tradition of the Reformation, Bonhoeffer insists on the word character of revelation and on the place that the church affords the proclamation of the Word accordingly (cf. *CS*, 160-61).

In 1940 this constituted for him not a dead tradition but a living reality. In the spring of that year, while German troops rolled over Europe in an

---

2. Cf. Bethge, *Dietrich Bonhoeffer*, 361: "At first, it seemed very strange to his students that their sermons, however hesitant and wanting, were treated in all seriousness as the expression of the true *viva vox Christi*."

orgy of high-powered action, Bonhoeffer sang the "glory of the Word." "What meaning can the word of the church still have in a world in which actions speak their own language so overwhelmingly? Has that word not become superfluous? Should we not simply join in those actions and, instead of all those words, just cooperate? Actions possess credibility." That is the beginning of the text of which only a fragment has been preserved. Bonhoeffer comments that church people have also contributed to the power of actions that has drowned out the word of the church. They have collaborated with the hegemony of actions. "Actions carry their own weight. Without a word they roll over everything that is weaker than they. They let it lie and trample on it. . . . That is the immanent law of actions" (GS, 3:416).

In the midst of this historical praise of actions Bonhoeffer nevertheless keeps asking about the Word of God. He attributes to it unsuspected power. "The Word of God is there and it is the only thing that an action has no power over. The human powers that surround the Word of God may be slight and weak so that they may be broken and destroyed. Only the Word of God endures. . . . In actions God remains mute, but God reveals himself to those whom God wants to save, those who might find God. That revelation occurs in the poverty of the word, for God wants to be *believed*, not to gain recognition by force. Rather God wills the Word to affect the heart and lead it to a free belief" (GS, 3:417). We know Bonhoeffer (especially from *Cost of Discipleship*) primarily as one who reproaches belief for its lack of powerful action and for its excess of verbalism. Here we encounter him as one who in the line of Luther and Barth elevates the weakness of human words to a locus of the power of God. God communicates with human beings within ear range and at eye level, taking them completely seriously in their humanity.

The church lives by the Word and proclaims it in the expectation that where the Word of God is preached, it is God who will speak. "Praedicatio verbi divini est verbum divinum" (the preaching of the Word of God is the Word of God). Bonhoeffer subscribes to this confession, which goes back to Heinrich Bullinger (1504-1575) and which has been included in the confession of the Lutheran Church (CS, 161). Bonhoeffer entered into the service of that church contrary to the expectations of his environment and despite the dissuasion of his family. He began his theological career by proclaiming the Word each Sunday in the German congregation of Barcelona (where he was curate in 1928). In a sermon on April 15, 1928, on the promise of Christ, "See, I am with you always, even to the end of the age"

(Matt. 28:20), he tells what he expects of proclamation. He interprets his Bible text as follows. "Jesus is with us in his Word. . . . In our dealings with the Word of Jesus we experience his nearness. A word is the clearest and most distinct means of expression by which spiritual beings have contact with each other. When we have the word of a human being, then we know the will and the person of that being. When we have the Word of Jesus, then we know his will and the whole of his person. . . . Our whole life stands under his word and is sanctified by his word." Without further explanation or argumentation Bonhoeffer then confers the authority of the Word of Jesus to the proclamation of the church. "From baptism to the grave the word of the church accompanies a human being, placing one under the assurance of the word, 'See, I am with you.' As a symbol of this the church has placed the decisive periods of life under its proclamation" (*GS*, 5:431; *DBW*, 10:471). The faithful word of the church *is* the Word of God.

The notion that the word of the church will be so omnipresent that it will encompass and permeate each human existence in every phase of life accompanies Bonhoeffer's initial high expectations of the proclamation of the Word. In that context the Sunday sermon is a central, but not exclusive, means. In Finkenwalde Bonhoeffer also points to pastoral care as a form of proclamation.[3] The basis of pastoral care is not meddlesomeness by the church or religious totalitarianism, but the belief that in proclamation God wants to be present among human beings. That conviction made of Bonhoeffer, the academic theologian, a congregational preacher, one who preached often and gladly, whether in Barcelona, Berlin, London, Finkenwalde, or in the concentration camp of Flossenbürg, the day before his death.[4] Later he would probably have toned down his farewell sermon from his first congregation in Barcelona in 1928, but he would still subscribe to the essence of it. "It is a great thing," he told his congregation, having served it for a year, "to have to speak about God and to know at the same time that with human words one can at the most touch the seam of God's holy robe, and that it is God's grace when God should want to do something with it to God's own glory" (*GS*, 5:483; *DBW*, 10:539).

In the preface to a volume in which most of Bonhoeffer's sermons were brought together (*GS*, 4), Bethge defends the viewpoint that it would

---

3. "Caring for the soul is a special sort of proclamation" (*SC*, 30).

4. Sixty-three sermons of Bonhoeffer have been preserved. Fifty-six have been published.

be a misunderstanding to think that Bonhoeffer, with his final "non-religious" explorations, could be called on as a chief witness against preaching. To be sure, the baptismal sermon will lower the pulpit a great deal, but it will not break it down completely. Bethge points out how the *Christus praedicatus* (proclaimed Christ) remains the starting point of Bonhoeffer's theological endeavor from beginning to end. Later Bonhoeffer again raises the question, "Who is Christ for us today?" and concludes that the church has been driven from the center of culture and is no longer capable of reaching the hearts of modern humanity with its word. But even then he retains the insistence that Christ, albeit interpreted in terms of a "non-religious" context, must be proclaimed (cf. *LPP*, 285-86). Bethge concludes that preaching remained a constant focus in all of Bonhoeffer's theological development. "Discipleship, sympathy, silence, worldliness, all of that is no substitute for a sermon, but stands at the service of its enthronement" (*GS*, 4:9).

Bonhoeffer remained a preacher until the end, even if one might ask if he still wanted to stand in the pulpit of his church. In a sermon from 1932 he formulated in a striking image the high-spun ideal to which he wanted to measure preaching up to the end. "One cannot understand and preach the gospel tangibly enough. A truly evangelical sermon must be like offering a child a red apple or a thirsty person a glass of cool water and asking, 'Do you want it?' We should talk about matters of faith in such a manner that people would stretch out their hands for it faster than we can fill them" (*GS*, 4:51; *DBW*, 11:427).

The question whether one should proclaim the gospel was never an issue for Bonhoeffer. The question was how, when, and where. In Finkenwalde he developed a theory of preaching that sought to answer those questions for the 1930s. In prison that theory would be sharpened. We want to look more closely at this question now.

5.2 "It Is Christ Who Is the Word" (Lectures on Homiletics, 1935-39)

The lectures on homiletics, of which only notes by students have been preserved, encompass a period of four years. We find historical and biblical backgrounds as well as practical tips for the Sunday sermon. Bonhoeffer begins by placing preaching in a direct apostolic line with the proclamation of the gospel. Concepts like *martyrein* (to witness), *keryssein* (to preach), *euangelizein* (to evangelize) come in review. For Bonhoeffer, preaching is their contemporary form. The church still does what the apostles did. In their witness they were the "media" of the gospel that becomes reality in the church's proclamation of Christ (see 2.2).

Bonhoeffer lays the theological foundation of preaching in ecclesiology, the doctrine of the church. That relation he derives from the incarnation. In this we hear the theological heartbeat of his homiletics. Bonhoeffer advances the formulation that "the proclaimed word is the incarnate Christ himself. . . . It is the Christ himself walking through his congregation as the Word" (*WP*, 126). The seemingly massive identification between preaching and Christ, human word and Word of God, can only be understood against the background of Bonhoeffer's heavily loaded concept of the church that he developed in *Communion of Saints*. For Bonhoeffer the church is "Christ existing as community." It is the actualized form of the ultimate Word of God, the body of Jesus Christ. The word of the church is equivalent to that of Christ, because its body is equivalent to his. Such a reference to the incarnation must be properly understood. Preaching must not be seen as a continuation or repetition, a second realization of the incarnation, as once appeared to be the case with the sacrament in the Roman Catholic tradition, but as the *actualization* by the Holy Spirit of the incarnation realized once and for all in Christ (*CS*, 115-36). In the here and now of the proclaimed Word the Spirit actualizes for us the unique *Deus dixit* (God has spoken), Christ.

The *Christus praedicatus* (proclaimed Christ) is thus the *Christus praesens* (present Christ).

> The word of the sermon intends to accept humankind, nothing else. It wants to bear the whole of human nature. In the congregation all sins should be cast upon the Word. Preaching must so be done that the hearers place all of their needs, cares, fears, and sins upon the Word. That Word accepts all of these things. When preaching is done in this way, it is the proclamation of Christ. This proclamation of the Christ does not regard its primary responsibility to be giving advice, arousing emotions, or stimulating the will — it will do these things, too — but its intention is to sustain us. The Word is there that burdens might be laid upon it. We are all borne up by the Word of Christ. Because it does so, it creates fellowship. Because the Word includes us into itself, it makes us members of the body of Christ. As such we share in the responsibility of uphold-

ing one another. Thus the Word of Christ also presupposes Christian community. The Word intends that no one should remain alone, for in him no one remains alone (*WP*, 127, translation slightly altered).

What is striking is the pastoral tone that pervades Bonhoeffer's thoughts on the word. The word sustains and creates community. That concern has its source in the christological analogy that Bonhoeffer inserts in his views on the divine Word. Just as Christ, the realized Word, sustains us and holds our place for us, so also in the actualization of the Word.[5]

Bonhoeffer qualifies preaching theologically from the very beginning. God is the one who speaks. The Word comes from the other side, even if it is spoken by human beings. We hear several times of the spontaneous movement that characterizes the Word (*WP*, 128, 135, 169). The primary subject of the dynamics of preaching is not the preacher and his religious sentiment but God. "With the introduction of the biblical word the text begins moving among the congregation. Likewise the word arises out of the Bible, takes shape as the sermon, and enters into the congregation in order to bear it up." Bonhoeffer seems to want to elevate the divine Word so high above our own language ability and usage of speech that one questions whether anyone would ever be able to utter it. He admits readily that it is not something human that takes place there. "The form of the preached word is different from every other form of speech. . . . Human words communicate something else besides what they are of themselves. They become means to an end. The meaning of the proclaimed Word, however, does not lie outside of itself; it is the thing itself. It does not transmit anything else, it has no external objectives — rather it communicates that it is itself: the historical Jesus Christ, who bears humanity upon himself with all its sorrows and its guilt. The sustaining Christ is the dimension of the preached Word" (*WP*, 128). The Word of God is unique in its unbroken performativity. It possesses a quality that human words have long lost. It realizes what it says. It effectuates its own truth. It makes Christ and his salvation present (see 2.2).[6] The proclaimed Christ is the real and present Christ.

How can this Word ever be uttered by human beings? Does not Bonhoeffer, by beginning so high and divinely, deprive himself of the pos-

5. Cf. *CD*, 79ff., 98-99. "For God is a God who *bears*" (*CD*, 82).
6. Cf. *CD*, 52: "The call to follow at once produces a new situation." Ibid., 54: "It is only the call which creates the situation."

sibility of ever bringing the Word of God within human reach? Yet he extols in this context the dignity of human words as the full sustainer of the divine Word: "Nothing is equal in dignity to the spoken word" (*WP,* 128). But he immediately adds that the spoken word derives its dignity not from itself but from God. It can only sustain the message of God because it in turn is also *accepted* and *sustained* by the Word of Christ. The dignity of the word does not lie in its intrinsic qualities, but is attributed to it from outside. It derives its status from the incarnation of God in Christ. The content of proclamation can be nothing else than a *witness* to the Word of Christ, a witness that points away from itself to him. But even if the glory of the preaching be a conferred glory, it is still a glory. The word that is preached must be frank about that. The church must give the spoken word a central place in its worship, and not music, symbols, mystery, cult, or drama (*WP,* 127).[7] The word takes hold of people at the center of their will. It convicts them and places them under the promise. In that way it is the proper means for a confrontation with the gospel that commands and promises on behalf of God.

Despite the difference in quality and import between the Word of God and human words Bonhoeffer remains of the opinion that the Word of God can fully resound in the form of a human word. That can happen, however, only if preaching takes as its starting point the biblical witness. The original creative power of God remains present in proclamation, because the Bible witnesses to the fact that in Christ the Word of God and human words are again joined together. "Through the Word the world was created. The Word became incarnate. The incarnate Word continues to exist for us in the Scripture. Through the Holy Spirit, the incarnate Word comes to us from the Scripture in the sermon. And it is one and the same Word: the Word of creation, the Word of the incarnation, the Word of the Holy Scripture, the Word of the sermon. It is the creating, accepting, and reconciling Word of God, for whose sake the world exists" (*WP,* 129). In Bonhoeffer's views on preaching there are thus four forms of the Word of God. The creative and sustaining Word of God is the first and primary form. There is then the incarnate Word of Christ. The third is the biblical

---

7. Cf. *WP,* 168: "Because the spoken word in the Lutheran Church does not present a mystery or a holy drama as in the Roman Church — that is, it does not represent something else, but rather is the thing itself — therefore it has a particular significance for the Lutheran Church. . . . In its spoken form the Word is the specific central point of our church."

witness. Finally, there is proclamation in which the first three are actualized in the present.

Like Luther, Bonhoeffer understands the word of preaching to be a *verbum efficax* (effective word), which has received the original performative power that a common word in our fallen creation lacks. In proclamation God brings us back in contact with our origin, the creative Word from the beginning. And God's Word does not return empty (Isa. 55:11). "It is truth that has taken place. It creates its own form of existence" (*WP*, 139). In this context Bonhoeffer coins a term (and I return to it at the end of this chapter) for this self-actualizing salvific character of the divine Word. There is, he says, a *sacramentum verbi* (sacrament of the word) (*WP*, 130). Just as salvation is present and sealed in the tangible and visible sacrament, so it is also concretely present in the audible word. The word of salvation makes salvation present. It is not a means to something else. It has no other goal than its own presence (*WP*, 169).

5.3 The "Rules of Language"

In the face of so massive a theological argumentation the contemporary reader will likely tend to cry out whether it might not be toned down a little. In the biography Bethge also relativizes the high-pitched tone of Bonhoeffer's homiletics and excuses its self-assurance a little by emphasizing the context of the time in which it was developed, the church struggle of the 1930s. There seems to be no trace of uncertainty or hesitation. The misgivings with regard to the liberating power of proclamation, which pervade the baptismal sermon, seem to be a matter of a later date. The hearer, "non-religious" and "come of age," whom Bonhoeffer then wants to let have a say, seems in the homiletics still to be condemned to silence. In the midst and in the face of National Socialism the church had to sound a robust and firm note. "In Christ there is no place for conditional sentences," Bonhoeffer told his students in Finkenwalde. It was not the time for a subtle hermeneutic. In the thick of the church struggle, at the end of 1933, he wrote to Martin Niemöller, "Today only the language of Luther and not of Melanchthon helps" (*TF*, 416).[8] Bethge concludes: "It was both

---

8. Cf. *GS*, 1:206 (letter to Bishop Amudsen of August 8, 1934): "we have to go into it and get through it, without the diplomatics of open Christian talk."

the strength and the weakness of these homiletics that they were so exactly adapted to the thirties."[9]

Still one must ask whether Bonhoeffer really needs to be protected from himself. Are his views on speaking about God so contextually determined? The suggestion that his homiletics is based on the same sort of a positivism of revelation for which he later reproached Barth is, in my opinion, incorrect. Dietrich Bonhoeffer is no Eduard Thurneysen, who so emphasized the Word of God in preaching that he paid no attention at all to its human form. Even if Bonhoeffer defended a high-strung theology of the Word of God, he surrounded it with so much care and placed so many conditions on it that there can be no question of a massive fetishism of the Word. That he sounded a different tone in the baptismal sermon probably derives not from his having altered his views on the Word of God, but from the fact that the conditions under which they might become effective were less present.

One might mistake the theological identification of the word of proclamation with the Word of God as permission for a careless and arbitrary usage of words and language. If it is God who speaks from the pulpit, who would dare call God to account? Homiletics that have been developed from the point of view of dialectical theology have often severely violated the rules of communication by appealing to theological immunity.[10] But that is not the case with Bonhoeffer. He takes a different viewpoint. If Protestantism focuses attention on the Word, "our speaking is open to danger and must be disciplined. Because the Word is able to triumph, reign, and comfort, it is necessary for us to recognize the rules of language, learn what they are, and follow them" (*WP*, 168). Because Bonhoeffer thinks so radically in terms of the incarnation, he wants theology to consult linguistics and communication sciences. If the Word has become flesh, then it has at the least become language and, therefore, shares its conditions. In that respect what one finds concretely by Bonhoeffer is minimal. How could it be otherwise under the circumstances of the time? But the intention is there, even if Bonhoeffer does

9. Bethge, *Dietrich Bonhoeffer*, 363.

10. Thurneysen's practical homiletics consisted of four (negative) rules: (1) use no rhetoric; (2) do not play to the desires of the hearer; (3) give no psychological encouragement; and (4) provide no variation in the sermon. See his essay "Der Aufgabe der Predigt" (The task of preaching) (1921), in *Aufgabe der Predigt* (The task of preaching), ed. G. Hummel (Darmstadt: Wissenschaftliche Buchgesellschaft, 1971), 105-18.

not get beyond setting a number of general conditions for the language of proclamation.

Bonhoeffer stands with his homiletics in a tradition that goes back to the Reformation. That tradition formulated the confession that "the proclamation of the divine Word *is* the divine Word" (see above and *CS*, 160). In his homiletics Bonhoeffer tries to do everything possible to prevent the preacher from letting that *is* be derailed, either from mistaken subjectivity or from mistaken objectivity. The preacher must not get in the way of God's Word, but must also not think that he can remain on the sideline. With regard to the first, Bonhoeffer advises the preacher to trust the autonomous dynamic of the Word of God ("seine Eigenbewegung und Kraft") and not rely on one's own religious virtuosity or rhetorical talent. "The Word does not need to be made alive. . . . In the proper sense, God is the one who speaks, not us. We must make room in every speech for the inherent purpose of the Word itself" (*WP*, 170). Is that not a license for shoddy arbitrariness and authoritarian pedantry? From what follows, it becomes clear that Bonhoeffer does not consider the identification, which none other than God enacted by shrouding the deity in the humble form of a human word, as ontological identity, but as a truth that is told on God's behalf. Only in that word being told is it true.

Bonhoeffer is at the least aware of the misuse that could be made of a reformational homiletics. "The fact that we are not identical with the actual One who brings the Word should be expressed both in the liturgy and in the sermon. Again, we may take as an example our being deeply involved in the reading of a letter which another has written. In secular speeches — for example, political speeches — everything hangs upon the discernible *identity* between the speaker and his words. In the delivery of the divine Word, however, everything depends upon the discernible *distance*. . . . Our humility with reference to the separation between ourselves and the Word is no virtue of ours; it is not a matter of a humble-sounding inflection, and it does not produce a particular type of preacher-personality. It is the only appropriate subjective attitude with reference to the Word" (*WP*, 170-71). With pertinent theological arguments Bonhoeffer makes a plea for a sense of awe in relation to the great Word of God. But do we not again see the Bonhoeffer family rising up in the background, where the same humility was practiced? Bonhoeffer impresses on his students that "the most extreme restraint and conciseness of language is appropriate for the sermon. Every superfluous word causes the Word to become inaudible among so many words" (*WP*, 174-75). We hear not only Dietrich Bonhoeffer but also Karl Bonhoeffer speaking.

The preacher must guard himself from a mistaken subjectivity. But there is also a mistaken objectivity. Proclamation is no mechanical automatism. "The Word intends that it should be spoken by a human being and not an institution" (*GS*, 4:279, slightly altered). The preacher who takes that into account is open to *genuine* subjectivity. In Bonhoeffer's description, one cannot avoid recalling the demands placed on speech in his family: "Pastors should, and can, serve the congregation as the persons they really are, with their individuality. Here the concept of genuineness becomes important, a genuineness which is committed to service and is disciplined (Col. 2:23). Everything unnatural and artificial hinders the preacher's credibility and stands as a lie in the way of the Word. It is unnatural to prevent naturalness. Genuineness is the opposite of pretentiousness and of the attitude of 'letting one's self go.' . . . If humility is the proper attitude for the speaker with reference to God and God's Word, then genuineness, in its truest sense, is the proper attitude for the speaker with reference to the congregation" (*WP*, 172). Naturalness, tact, and simplicity were the qualities, the conditions, that had to be met among the Bonhoeffers. Here we find them again, almost literally, but now as standards for speaking about God. Now, however, the reasons are theological. A theology from the point of view of incarnation must respect the "laws of language."

Lastly Bonhoeffer warns of a misunderstanding that could arise under so much humility. Let no one think that humility is the same as timidity. "We are witnesses, not the trumpeters of the Last Judgment" (*WP*, 173). With that word he admonishes the preacher to use words with dignity and to avoid a false passion. But that does not mean that the preacher as a reaction can completely erase himself. One may also notice that he is present. Was it not so that the Bonhoeffers also appreciated straightforwardness and self-confidence when one spoke? One recognizes the same values in Bonhoeffer's homiletic. "The Word of God demands a great deal of reserve and awe, but it demands an even greater confidence and joyfulness in its power and might" (*WP*, 173).

One can conclude that Bonhoeffer defended a high-pitched theology of the Word, but that he did not use it as an alibi for verbal violence or arbitrariness. He demonstrated that he was aware of the derailments, the dangers, and the limits of the spoken word.

5.4 Waiting for the Word
(A Meditative Approach to the Bible)

That awareness can be illustrated by the meditative approach that Bon-hoeffer as a preacher took to the Bible. We have seen that he had four "forms" of the Word of God in his views on preaching. There is (1) the creative and sustaining Word of God, (2) the incarnate Word in Christ, (3) the biblical witness, and finally (4) the proclamation in which the former three are actualized. We find little on their interrelatedness in Bonhoeffer's exposition that Barth did not handle more thoroughly and with greater clarity. "Scriptura est verbum dei" (Scripture is the Word of God). From the very beginning Bonhoeffer followed Barth in this (not unproblematic) identification. He advocated a theological interpretation of the Bible that did not deny the importance of historical-critical research on the origins of the text for exegesis, but he did not want to stop there. For him, as it was for Luther, the center of Scripture is Christ, and everything in the Bible must be read and judged by the question "What promotes Christ?" ("Was Christum treibet?").[11] Bonhoeffer read the Bible primarily as the book of the church. He sounded out and listened to the words of the text for the sake of the revealed Word of the God who speaks, Christ. Bonhoeffer called such a reading a "theological interpretation": "Theological exposition takes the Bible as the book of the church and interprets it as such." That is the way Bonhoeffer formulates it at the beginning of *Creation and Fall*, his first attempt at theological exegesis of the first three chapters of Genesis (*CF*, 22). "This word, spoken and heard as a human word, is the form of a servant in which from the beginning God encounters us and in which alone God wills to be found" (*CF*, 30).

Even though Bonhoeffer was well trained at the University of Berlin in the application of the historical-critical method, in his student years he already rebelled against his teachers, under the influence of the writings of Barth and Thurneysen, by advocating what he called a "pneumatic exegesis." By that he meant an interpretation of the Bible that derives its principles only from Scripture itself. The relation to the Reformation is in that way restored. The Reformation postulated that Scripture is its own interpreter ("scriptura sacra est sui ipsius interpres"). "No one can any longer

---

11. "His conviction was that the entirety of Scripture proclaims the one Lord, who calls to follow" (M. Kuske and I. Tödt, *DBW*, 4:9).

neglect historical criticism," Bonhoeffer recognized as a young student in 1925.[12] But the Spirit and not the letter, God and not our own subjectivity, lets the Bible truly speak to us. "Pneumatic exegesis" grounds itself in revelation, in the principle that only God can interpret God. Even if it recognizes that the Word of God has shrouded itself in the flesh of a human word, that the Word lies hidden in human words, only God can say that to us (*DBW*, 10:308ff.). Bonhoeffer learned to read the Bible as the Word of God directed to us, as "God's revealed word for all peoples, for all times" (*LT*, 60).

Bonhoeffer drew on the principle of revelation not only for his conception of preaching but also for his views on the Bible and the canon of Scripture. What is the relation then of his pneumatic or, as he would later call it, his theological exegesis to the historical-critical method? One thing is clear. However critical Bonhoeffer was of the latter form of biblical interpretation, he wanted to have nothing to do with a fundamentalist appeal to a literal "verbal inspiration" (*CC*, 73). But how can the text be granted space and independence to have its own say if from the beginning it is subordinated to revelation? Bonhoeffer was not able to resolve this in 1925; he could not clarify the relation between text and revelation, word and Word. From his teacher Reinhold Seeberg he received only an average grade ("satisfactory") on his paper on "historical and pneumatic exegesis." But did he ever do better? One can with reason question that. There was no one who later would declare misplaced the indignation of biblical scholars like Friedrich Baumgärtel and Gerhard von Rad against Bonhoeffer's attempts in the 1930s at a "theological interpretation of the Old Testament." His studies on the Psalms and of Ezra and Nehemiah are not examples of careful, scholarly exegesis, but are clearly at the service of the cause of the Confessing Church. In those years exegesis was for Bonhoeffer equivalent to war. Consequently, he sometimes took the text for a ride. At times, Bonhoeffer seemed to lack scholarly care and respect for the written word. His students in Finkenwalde admitted what he did not want to recognize. "Bonhoeffer was determined to make the texts speak to our time . . . and for that end every help and every commentator was welcome."[13]

12. Cf. *CC*, 74: "We must get into the troubled waters of historical criticism."
13. Wilhelm Rott, in Zimmermann and Smith, *I Knew Dietrich Bonhoeffer*, 133-34. Cf. the critical judgment by Wendel, *Studien*, 96-97: "For historically and scholarly controlled thinking the whole thing is a not reproducible transgression." Cf. Hans-Dirk van Hoogstraten, *Interpretatie: Een onderzoek naar de veranderingen in het denken van*

In that respect one need not take Bonhoeffer as an example. He did, however, seek to bind the preacher to the Bible. In his lectures on homiletics we read: "When we ask ourselves, 'What shall I say today to the congregation?' we are lost. But when we ask, 'What does this text say to the congregation?' we find ample support and abundant confidence" (*WP*, 158).[14] There are others who say the same, for whom, in the line of Barth, proclamation coincides with exegesis, exegesis, and again exegesis. Here, however, I emphasize that Bonhoeffer placed his own accent by the spiritual manner in which he handled the same theological concept. His meditative way of approaching Scripture was so characteristic for him that others perceived it as an uncritical form of naiveté. Even his students were sometimes amazed at his biblical piety. An example is Joachim Kanitz, who was told by Bonhoeffer that he "was not to forget that every word of Holy Scriptures is a love letter from God, directed entirely and personally to us."[15] For Bonhoeffer the Bible was certainly the Word of God. He did not experience that as an abstract principle, however, but as a living, intimate reality.

In a letter from 1936 to his brother-in-law Rüdiger Schleicher, who just like other members of the family must have raised his eyebrows once in a while at Dietrich's Christian radicalism in those years, he explains how he thinks about the Bible. Whoever hears Bonhoeffer say that "only the Bible has an answer to all our questions" might suspect the worst simplism. But he adds immediately that we have to ask "insistently" and "with humility" in order to receive an answer from it. That modest tone and the subtlety that accompanies it are now familiar to us. When in the rest of the letter Bonhoeffer explains his dealings with the Bible, it becomes apparent how he carries on a conversation with it with the same respect as with a

---

Dietrich Bonhoeffer en naar de consequenties daarvan voor de vertolking van de bijbel (Interpretation: An inquiry into the changes in the thought of Dietrich Bonhoeffer and into their consequences for the interpretation of the Bible) (Assen: Van Gorcum, 1973), 95-103.

14. In the choice of a text Bonhoeffer allowed the preacher freedom. "The freedom in the choice of a text is . . . at the service of the entirety of the witness to Christ." A sermon does not have to fit the text as long as it fits Scripture (*GS*, 3:321, "The Interpretation of the New Testament"). In that loose dealing with the text a certain legitimation of the subjective and temporal experience of the preacher can be ascertained. For Bonhoeffer Rom. 12:11, "Serve the time" (according to some manuscripts), was the great motto of preaching (*CS*, 161; cf. *DBW*, 10:512; Wendel, *Studien*, 25, 29, 41; Bethge, *Dietrich Bonhoeffer*, 81). At certain times there are texts one cannot preach on (*WP*, 159).

15. Quoted by Wendel, *Studien*, 80.

living person, for "in the Bible God speaks to us. And we cannot simply reflect upon God from ourselves; rather we must ask him. Only when we seek him does he answer. Naturally one can also read the Bible like any other book as, for example, from the viewpoint of textual criticism, etc. There is certainly nothing to be said against this. Only that it is not the way that reveals the essence of the Bible, only its superficial surface. Just as we do not grasp the word of a person whom we love, in order to dissect it; but just as such a word is simply accepted, and it then lingers with us all day long, simply as the word of this person whom we love, and just as the one who reveals himself to us as the one who has spoken to us in this word that is moving us ever more deeply in our hearts like Mary, so should we treat the Word of God" (*TF*, 425; translation slightly altered).

Bonhoeffer uses conversation as a metaphor for his interpretation of the Bible. He says that reading is like a dialogical exchange of question and answer. By doing so he places himself in the line of hermeneutics from Schleiermacher to Gadamer. In light of modern hermeneutics one could say that Bonhoeffer supposed too innocently that the meaning of a text lies in the intention of the author. But I point to the fact that, in his treatment of the Bible, Bonhoeffer applied the same dialectic of silence and speaking, openness and reticence, concealment and disclosure, that he attributed to personal conversation. Just as with respect to another person, we should not want to intrude impatiently and analytically on that person, so too with the Bible, one does not pluck the flower in its budding. We have to learn the art of attentively waiting, so that God will yield the mystery of his Word. God's Word takes time as well (see 3.4). Such a treatment of the Bible seems to require an "art of conversation," which at the least must meet the same conditions as a common, personal conversation. From *Life Together*, Bonhoeffer's record for posterity of the communal years in Finkenwalde, it becomes clear that "patience" and "waiting" also belong to the rules for dealing with Scripture. In the passage where Bonhoeffer recommends a daily time of meditation, he defines it emphatically as *Bible* meditation. "This time for meditation does not allow us to sink into the void and bottomless pit of aloneness, rather it allows us to be alone with the Word." One who meditates reads the Bible differently from one who stands in the pulpit or at a lectern, namely, as "God's Word for me personally. We expose ourselves to the particular sentence and word until we personally are affected by it. . . . We are reading God's Word as God's Word for us. . . . In this situation we are not doing an exegesis of the text, nor prepar-

ing a sermon or conducting a Bible study of any kind; we are rather waiting for God's Word to us. We are not waiting in vain; on the contrary, we
are waiting on the basis of a clear promise" (*LT,* 86-87).

It seems that the situation Bonhoeffer would later describe in the
baptismal sermon as holding generally for the entire church is sketched
here on a personal scale. The same elements are present. On the one hand,
there are the words of God that want to affect us, but that do not yield their
mystery. On the other hand, there is an attitude of waiting, a waiting that
will not be in vain because it is fed by a promise. In the baptismal sermon
the time of that "waiting for the redeeming word" is filled with among
other things silence and prayer. The section on daily meditation in *Life Together* also insists on silence in meditation as a means of strengthening
one's prayer life. In the words with which Bonhoeffer describes it he almost literally quotes his own letter to Rüdiger Schleicher, three years before. "It is not necessary for us to be anxious about putting our thoughts
and prayers into words as we meditate. Silent thinking and prayer, which
comes only from our listening, can often be more beneficial. It is not necessary for us to find new ideas in our meditation. It is perfectly sufficient if
the Word enters in and dwells within us as we read and understand it. As
Mary 'pondered . . . in her heart' what the shepherds told her [Luke 2:19],
as a person's words often stick in our mind for a long time — as they dwell
and work within us, preoccupy us, disturb us, or make us happy without
our being able to do anything about it — so we meditate, God's Word desires to enter in and stay with us. It desires to move us, to work in us and to
make such an impression on us that the whole day long we will not get
away from it. Then it will do its work in us, often without our being aware
of it" (*LT,* 88).

Even if Bonhoeffer in the baptism letter describes the situation of the
church in similar terms of patience, waiting, and silence, we cannot dispense with it as merely a stretched-out "meditation on a large scale." There
is more at stake, as we have seen (chap. 2). Still I am of the opinion that we
should confront the crisis of language that is described in the "Thoughts
for the Day of Baptism" less dramatically now that we have observed the
essential role that concepts like silence and waiting play in Bonhoeffer's
theological concept of the Word of God. Being compelled to silence does
not mean for Bonhoeffer the end of faith in a God who speaks; rather, it is
a constitutive part of it.

In *Life Together* Bonhoeffer even devotes a couple of pages to the relation of silence to the Word. I highlight a few passages. "Genuine speech comes out of silence, and genuine silence comes out of speech. Silence does not mean being incapable of speech, just as speech does not mean idle talk." Bonhoeffer describes Christian silence as a "silence under the Word and silence that comes out of the Word" (*LT*, 84). He recognizes that mysticism is familiar with silence, but he is nevertheless sharp in his criticism. Its silence is different, perhaps mistaken. "There is an indifferent or even negative attitude toward silence which sees in it a disparagement of God's revelation in the Word. Silence is misunderstood as a solemn gesture, as a mystical desire to get beyond the Word. Silence is no longer seen in its essential relationship to the Word, as the simple act of the individual who falls silent under the Word of God. We are silent before hearing the Word because our thoughts are already focused on the Word, as children are quiet when they enter their father's room. . . . In the end, silence means nothing other than waiting for God's Word and coming from God's Word with a blessing." Bonhoeffer wanted by all means to keep silence within the sphere of influence of speech, as a humble, listening silence. It is an intermission of the Word, not a transgression of its limits. The issue is not silence in itself,[16] but "silence in conjunction with the Word" (*LT*, 84-85). It is a silence that considers stillness not to be the holy of holies but essential to an encounter with the holy.

Bonhoeffer wanted to have every instance of speaking of God preceded by such an encounter in silence with the Bible. In his homiletics he suggested that the preacher who prepares a sermon first enter into prayer and meditation before the exegetical analysis of the text (*WP*, 145-46). The one who can listen speaks differently as well. To quote *Life Together* again, "silence before the Word leads to proper hearing and thus also to proper speaking of God's Word at the right time. Much that is unnecessary remains unsaid. But what is essential and helpful can be said in a few words" (*LT*, 85).

---

16. "Silence can be a dreadful wasteland with all its isolated stretches and terrors. It can also be a paradise of self-deception. One is not better than the other. Be that as it may, let no one expect from silence anything but a simple encounter with the Word of God for the sake of which Christians have entered into silence" (*LT*, 86).

5.5 Out of the Pulpit (Lectures on
Spiritual Care, 1935-39)

Bonhoeffer's theology of the Word does not appear to be all that massive. Even though he holds to all of its pretensions (everything is staked out on the redeeming Word), he gives an account of the conditions, limits, and dangers of the spoken word. That is apparent from the way a preacher is to deal with the Bible as described above, but also from Bonhoeffer's treatment of the hearer of the Word and the context of that hearer. In this respect I am of the opinion that in the baptism letter Bonhoeffer, rather than breaking with his theological concept of the Word of God, stretches it to its utmost limit. The importance afforded to the hearer of the Word in Bonhoeffer's theology reaches its high point in the letters from prison, but it has in fact already been prepared in his earlier writings. In homiletic theory in the line of dialectical theology, the hearer is reduced to silence, as already illustrated with reference to Thurneysen. Every word allowed of the hearer would be to the detriment of the divine Word. For Bonhoeffer that is much less the case.

In his lectures on *Spiritual Care* that he gave parallel to homiletics from 1935 to 1939 in Finkenwalde, he defends a broad conception of proclamation. Sunday preaching is one form of proclamation, and pastoral care another. Not just public proclamation but also a personal, caring conversation can be a medium of God's activity (see 3.4-5). Bonhoeffer does not narrow his theology of the Word down to the Sunday sermon.[17] At the same time he emphatically maintains a view of pastoral activity in the tradition of dialectical theology. For him pastoral care is at the service of proclamation. The focus of spiritual care is to lead an individual member of the church, who as a sinner is unable to hear the gospel, back to the word of grace. Bonhoeffer does not want to speak of "spiritual care as proclamation" (does he distance himself from Thurneysen?) but of "spiritual care as *diakonia*

---

17. Cf. Grözinger, *Die Sprache des Menschen* (Human language), 229, who observes how in the line of Barth "an immeasurably exaggerated concept of the sermon with homiletically catastrophic consequences" could arise. He quotes D. Rössler, "The sermon has to be everything that flows together in the formal concept of proclamation: kerygma and revelation, God's own Word, a past and at the same time a present salvation event. In that way the concept of the sermon and the Sunday task of the minister are burdened and loaded in an insurpassable manner" (ibid., 230).

[service]."[18] A specific sin in the life of a church member is responsible for that person's inability to hear the Word of God. It is the task of the pastor to bring that sin to light and to move the other to speak, to lead the hardened heart to confess sin to God and to lead the other back to "the loosing and binding Word" (SC, 40). The flight from the presence of the Word of God is at the heart of all problems. In that respect the pastor understands those facing him better than they understand themselves. We hear robust and firm language from a massive theology of the Word, and we see a concept of pastoral care being defended that in its fixation on a person as sinner is miles away from present-day conceptions that focus on giving help in life problems. We hear from Bonhoeffer that the relation of pastor and church member is one of "above and below," not next to each other. "The office of spiritual care does not exist to declare solidarity but to listen and to proclaim the gospel" (SC, 37).[19] Bonhoeffer advises his students in this context to walk through the streets with a big Bible under their arm, as he had observed Jean Laserre doing in northern France. "That is helpful because then everyone knows what's going on in the visitation" (SC, 47).

There is no point in further discussing this dated theory of spiritual care. I do want to point to a couple of elements that alleviate the possible monological, authoritarian character of this model of a theology of God's Word. First, it is devoid of a fixation on the pulpit. Bonhoeffer emphasizes that in his spiritual care a pastor must come down from the pulpit, making himself somewhat vulnerable by venturing out of the cover that chancel, altar, or vestment provides (SC, 45). The pastor is still sustained by the institutional protection that the context of ministry provides. He is the preacher, and he is expected to proclaim the gospel. But Bonhoeffer admits that in pastoral care no pastor can hide behind that. "All spiritual care transcends the medium of the pastor's personality" (SC, 51). The role that he plays is decisive, but that role has substance only because he, as a particular person, plays it. Personally he has to unravel the one Word for the specific situations of everyday life, there where other persons disclose themselves as they are (SC, 46).

---

18. Bonhoeffer does not refer explicitly to Thurneysen, but the parallels are clear. The relation between the two is worthy of further research. For the views on pastoral care of Thurneysen and the development within those views, see Gerben Heitink, *Pastoraat als hulpverlening* (Pastoral care as giving help) (Kampen: Kok, 1977), 136-44.

19. The hierarchy must be properly understood. "It is not a question of power relationships but of a difference in commission" (SC, 37).

In these last formulations one recalls directly what Bonhoeffer observed in prison. There he states that the people around him "as they are now simply cannot be religious any more" (*LPP,* 279). At that time he wants to acknowledge fully that experience in his theology, without being able or wanting to seek the authorization of the church. Here things have not yet gone so far. But the chinks through which a new wind will later blow through his theology are already visible here. In the context of a monological and objectivistic theology of the Word, there is no place for the subjective world of experience of both speaker and hearer. Bonhoeffer also draws attention to the fact that it is not the mission of pastors to "proclaim their experience, but to preach from Scripture. That can be proven and justified on the best theological grounds. Everything indeed depends on the Word" (*SC,* 68). But at the same time, it is noteworthy that Bonhoeffer speaks of a disturbing "misuse" of the Word, which occurs when "we have to say things we have not experientially discovered. . . . It's a sorry state of affairs if we are not bothered that our experience lags so far behind the Word, or if we strike the pose of martyrs who, renouncing their own experience, subjected themselves for the sake of proclaiming a strange Word. The peak of theological craftiness is to conceal necessary and wholesome unrest under such self-justification" (*SC,* 68).[20] Bonhoeffer shares the Barthian distrust of a theology that grants primacy to feelings in religion, but he is apparently just as wary of a theology that has lost contact with experience. He even calls that the "curse of theology." With Luther, he had previously, and perhaps ironically, characterized the situation in which the "whole Christian terminology is known and even respected" so that "it rolls out of our mouths without a hitch" as one of "temptation" (*SC,* 55).

The Word to be proclaimed is not up for grabs, nor can it be read directly from the Bible. It has to be born in the context of the pastoral situation. Here again Bonhoeffer is aware of the conditions and limits of the spoken word, and he calls on the pastors in training to observe them. I do not in the first place mean the official obligation to remain silent on confidential matters or the advice to consider well each word that they utter to their congregation, inasmuch as "the greatest vice in the congregation is usually gossip." Such dangers can be banned by a sermon once in a while on the "evils of the tongue" (*SC,* 40). Also I do not have in mind the "mod-

20. Cf. *SC,* 45: parishioners "can tell if our proclamation is a spiritual reality for us."

esty" and "extreme restraint" that Bonhoeffer ascribes to pastors making house calls or the recommendation not to waste time with small talk, under the motto, "He has no time for small talk, but he always has time to serve" (*SC*, 46). Both the fatherly figure of Karl Barth and that of Karl Bonhoeffer can be recognized in such practical tips for careful dealings with the Word. "Any 'Christian' exhibitionism must be guarded against from the beginning. Spiritual care is quite modest" (*SC*, 39). Hearing those words we can again easily recognize a Bonhoeffer family trait. Those practical recommendations give certain accents to his theology of the Word, without decisively coloring them.

What is decisive, however, is the importance Bonhoeffer attributes to silence in pastoral care. He sets a brake on the escape into verbalism as well as on the escape into authoritarianism. "We should not undersell or obscure the Word to anyone" (*SC*, 42). That maxim he wishes to see as a watchword in pastoral care. Spiritual care must also be possible with a closed mouth. "The pastor often accompanies the other person on pilgrimage silently and wordlessly, but at all times as intercessor" (*SC*, 38). Such a statement is at odds with the verbalism of certain forms of a theology of the Word. Also surprising in this context is the comment that when people are offended by the discrepancy between words and actions of a church or of a preacher, the best spiritual care is "the quiet service of love," a witness that "everyone understands" (*SC*, 50-51). In the baptismal sermon, written much later, we come across words of the same tenor about the language spoken by "doing justice," as long as the words of the church remain powerless.

In this context I point to elements in Bonhoeffer's views on pastoral care that take his theology of the Word away from the pulpit and pry it loose from the authority of the office of a minister of the Word. Bonhoeffer can imagine a complete change of roles in the pastoral situation, in which the speaker and the hearer of the Word of God exchange places. In "spiritual care as *diakonia*," which Bonhoeffer advocates, "the pastor's task is to listen and the parishioner's is to talk. The pastor's duty in this form of spiritual care may be to be silent for a long time" (*SC*, 31). That the silence can and must be broken is a supposition that Bonhoeffer does not let go of. It is a silence in the context of proclamation, in which spiritual care should eventually result. But it does not really matter which of the two, pastor or church member, breaks the silence. It might well be the church member. One of the reasons that Bonhoeffer considers spiritual care to be necessary is that it is essential for the church member to be able to speak, for which there is no opportunity in the sermon (*SC*, 32). In his version of the theology of the Word it is essential that the proclaimer be able to listen, for the sake of his proclamation. "Those who cannot hear another person are also no longer able to hear God's Word" (*SC*, 36).[21] The hearer plays a constitutive role in any speaking of the Word of God.

5.6 The Ears of God

In the lectures on spiritual care we do not hear much more about the theological significance that Bonhoeffer attributes to such listening. We do find it in the book *Life Together*, on which Bonhoeffer worked at the same time and in which a chapter is devoted to his view on "spiritual care as *diakonia*," but then under the more simple title "Service." There it can be seen how firmly Bonhoeffer roots the office of minister of the Word in the priesthood of all believers (*SC*, 32; cf. *CS*, 163). Ministry is for him a function of the life of the community. The preachers can stand over against the community with the Word, but only because they, as one of the members of the body of Christ, derive their mandate from the community.

In *Life Together* we read that in the context of the church the "service of the Word of God" is the last (in the sense of ultimate, highest) service that believers can render one another. The sermon from the pulpit is only a particular form of that service. Bonhoeffer thinks so highly of that service that he does not want to bind it to a specific office, but to consider it a task of every member of the Christian church. "This service has to do with the free word from person to person, not the word bound to a particular pastoral office, time, and place. It is a matter of that unique situation in which one person bears witness in human words to another person regarding all the comfort, the admonition, the kindness, and the firmness of God" (*LT*, 103). There, where speaking the Word of God cannot enjoy the shelter of an office under the authority of the institution of the church, it is essential to be aware of the conditions under which that Word can be effective. God should be spoken of in free conversation from one person to another. "The orderly word spoken in the pulpit is so much easier than this totally free word, stand-

---

21. Cf. *SC*, 31: "only after a long period of listening is one able to preach appropriately."

ing responsibly between silence and speech" (*LT,* 88). When Bonhoeffer sums up the conditions that such conversation has to meet, we see literally how the exclamation marks in his lectures on homiletics and spiritual care have been replaced by question marks. The high opinion he has of the "service of the Word" that people can render to each other makes it a precarious matter, in which the greatest caution must be observed.

It is the "last" service to which members of the body are called not just in the sense of highest, but also in time. They must first support each other by other services, before they can and may undertake the service of the Word.

> The *first* [to be understood in the sense of primary] service one owes to others in the community involves listening to them. Just as our love for God begins with listening to God's Word, the beginning of love for other Christians is learning to listen to them. God's love for us is shown by the fact that God not only gives us God's Word, but also lends us God's ear. We do God's work for our brothers and sisters when we learn to listen to them. So often Christians, especially preachers, think that their only service is always to have to "offer" something when they are together with other people. They forget that listening can be a greater service than speaking. Many people seek a sympathetic ear and do not find it among Christians, because these Christians are talking even when they should be listening. But Christians who can no longer listen to one another will soon no longer be listening to God either; they will always be talking even in the presence of God. The death of the spiritual life starts here, and in the end there is nothing left but empty spiritual chatter and clerical condescension which chokes on pious words. . . . For Christians, pastoral care differs essentially from preaching in that here the task of listening is joined to the task of speaking the Word. (*LT,* 98-99)

We have forgotten how to listen like that, Bonhoeffer observes. A sign of that is that we no longer maintain the practice of confession in the church. We know that Bonhoeffer greatly valued that custom and that he introduced its practice in Finkenwalde. The practical insight that we can help people by listening to them is in "secular spiritual care" more generally acknowledged than in the church, according to the judgment of the theologian Bonhoeffer, whose father had a flourishing psychiatric practice and who had grown up in an environment in which the mystery of every person was considered to be synonymous with "God" (see 3.4).

It is not just the practical and pastoral importance of listening that is intriguing here, but above all the theological dimension that Bonhoeffer attributes to it. "We should listen with the ears of God, so that we can speak the Word of God" (*LT*, 99). Speaking and silence are again dialectically related to each other. A theology of the Word looks a lot different when it begins not with speaking but with listening by God! Without being able to assert that Bonhoeffer relinquished his views on the profusion of the Word of God, I am of the opinion that the new theological insights that he formulates in the letters from prison are unthinkable without the readiness to listen. Listening was for Bonhoeffer not just a psychological wisdom but a theological necessity. Our listening takes as example the listening of God. One who adheres to such a theology has to allow oneself to be regularly interrupted, whether by working-class children in Berlin, persecuted Jews under Hitler, or nonreligious people in general. Such a theology of the Word is sensitive to the context, if not dependent on it.

I return for a moment to *Life Together*. Bonhoeffer insists that listening is the first service we owe one another. But it is not the only service before the service of the Word. The threshold of the Word lies still higher. The second service that Bonhoeffer discerns is the readiness to perform deeds of active helpfulness, simply being there for one another, ready to help when needed. The third is bearing one another's burdens. That entails enduring one another when the other becomes a burden. I will not go into those services further, but only observe that Bonhoeffer binds speaking about God to such stringent conditions that each word that one finally dares to say is a purified word. Who still dares to speak? When Bonhoeffer finally deals with that ultimate Word, we see a lot of question marks in his text.

> This word is threatened all about by endless dangers. If proper listening does not precede it, how can it really be the right word for the other? If it is contradicted by one's own lack of active helpfulness, how can it be a credible and truthful word? If it does not flow from the act of bearing with others, but from impatience and the spirit of violence against others, how can it be the liberating and healing word? On the contrary, the person who has really listened, served, and patiently borne with others is the very one who easily stops talking. A deep distrust of everything that is merely words often stifles a personal word to another Christian. What can a powerless human word accomplish for others? Why add to the empty talk? Are we, like those experienced spiritual "experts," to talk

past the real needs of the other person? What is more perilous than speaking God's Word superfluously? But, on the other hand, who wants to accept the responsibility for having been silent when we should have spoken? (*LT,* 103)

Bonhoeffer binds a Christian to the responsibility of keeping silent and speaking at the right moment, but he is unable to say when a Christian should do one or the other. No one can intrude by force into others (as we already read, in much the same language, in *Fiction from Prison*) and inflict harm on their own mysteries. But on the other hand, it is unchristian when one is unable to say a good word, thus denying the other "this decisive service." We hear not only Karl Bonhoeffer, but also Karl Barth speaking again through Bonhoeffer. We must not only respect the other's human dignity, but also see the other as a sinner, who when left only to that dignity will be lost (*LT,* 104-5). God "has put God's own Word in our mouth. God wants it to be spoken through us" (*LT,* 106).

I now conclude this section on Bonhoeffer's views on pastoral care. I have noted the tension that the presence of the hearer evokes in Bonhoeffer's theory of proclamation. The presence of the hearer does not mean the end of his theology of the Word and the resulting views on spiritual care, but it does place conditions on them that indicate their limitations. One finds them formulated in a personal outpouring in which Bonhoeffer shares his doubts about theology with his student friend Erwin Sutz. The letter was written early in 1932, when alongside his lecturing at the university Bonhoeffer attempted to do social work among young people in a working-class neighborhood of Berlin. In that context he also visited the parents of the boys with whom he worked. The experiences he had there appeared to make him feel somewhat inadequate to the challenge.

I sometimes, indeed often, stand there and think that I would have been as well equipped to do such visits if I had studied chemistry. It sometimes seems to me that all our work comes to grief on the care of souls. To think of those excruciating hours or minutes when I or the other person try to begin a pastoral conversation, and how haltingly and lamely it goes on! And in the background there are always the ghastly home conditions, about which one really cannot say anything. . . . In short, it is a very troubled chapter, and I sometimes try to console myself by thinking that this sort of pastoral care is something which just wasn't there before. But perhaps it is really the end of our Christianity that we fail here.

We have learnt to preach again, at least a little bit, but the care of souls?
(*NRS*, 151-52; partly in *TF*, 406)

The dilemma that Bonhoeffer faces here one can recognize in the light of what I have said. In the radicalization of his theology of the Word, which is to be of value not just from the pulpit but in every situation of life, he encounters the limits of its possibilities. Either he must label such a view on spiritual care, developed in the line of Barth, as "unchristian" and create a different theology that under no condition allows for an identification of God's Word and human words, or he must recognize that he fails as one who speaks the Word of God in situations of social crisis. Bonhoeffer seems to assume that it is the latter, much to his chagrin. His theology of the Word began with an exclamation mark. From now on it will be punctuated with a question mark. From Barth he learned how to preach again. But what if speaking as a Christian about God is not to be tested primarily in the pulpit, but as here, in a poor neighborhood of Berlin? The question remains and will again become clearly audible in prison (see 6.1).

5.7 Qualified Silence

Bonhoeffer bound speaking about God to stringent conditions, if it is to be presented as a speaking that comes from God. That he thus approached the limits of his theological model was something that he noticed not only in his views on spiritual care but also in his ethics. For the Lutheran Bonhoeffer, the proclamation of the Word had two forms, law and gospel. Christian ethics could in that context be seen as an element of proclamation. And, according to Bonhoeffer, ethics is the doctrine of the proclamation of the commandment of God. The Word of God resounds from the pulpit not only as a promise of salvation but also in concrete instruction on how to act with regard to good and evil.

Bonhoeffer had not always defended this pretentious view of ethics. In Barcelona he followed Barth's *Epistle to the Romans* and considered ethical actions by a Christian to be a demonstration of thankfulness for God's grace, not a concretization of God's Word. There are no generally valid principles of Christian action, but what God wants of us in a concrete situation is told to us at the moment. In the risk of our decision at that moment we hope that we do what is good in God's eyes and entrust our actions to God's grace.[22] That modified "situationism" would remain in Bonhoeffer's ethics. The more that National Socialism appealed to orders of creation for its ideology of "Blut und Boden" (blood and soil), the more Bonhoeffer distrusted creation as a source of general principles in ethics. Like Barth and the Confessing Church, Bonhoeffer drew back more and more to Christ for his argumentation in matters of ethics. But the change in his ethics that I want to point to is something different. The more the church of the 1930s felt the pinch of ethical problems, the more Bonhoeffer looked for a basis for Christian ethics that went further than a quasi-existentialist "God blessing the attempt." When the Word of God is a word that, "performatively," creates its own reality and when that Word must be proclaimed by human tongues (a position that Bonhoeffer defended, as we have seen), then that must hold not just for the gospel but also for the law, not just for God's promise but also for God's commandment.

In the early 1930s Bonhoeffer became involved in the upcoming ecumenical movement. Matters of war and armaments were at the top of the agenda. Should the world disarm itself, while Germany is rearming? Is pacifism God's commandment for the hour at hand (as Bonhoeffer initially believed) or just the contrary? How can God's Word be spoken in the moral dilemma of the concrete situation? In lectures at the University of Berlin, in ecumenical addresses, as well as in letters to his friend Erwin Sutz in 1932, we see Bonhoeffer wrestling with those questions. Ultimately he wants to judge the importance of all his theology from that vantage point. In August of 1932 he writes to Sutz, "In fact everything depends on the problem of ethics, that is, on the question of the possibility of the church proclaiming the concrete commandment. . . . It seems to me that for theological thought this is simply the first question and the starting point for all the rest" (*GS*, 1:33-34).

The ethical question, for Bonhoeffer, was not one of "application" or later "concretization" of a previous Word of God that we could derive from the Bible apart from that Word. Bonhoeffer argued that the Word of God is a dynamic and effective active word (*Tatwort*), as we have seen (4.4). It carries its effect with it. That is, it is concrete in this situation or it is not the Word of God. Bonhoeffer bound not only his homiletics but also his ethics to that stringent requirement. In the same letter to Sutz he confesses:

22. Cf. "What Is a Christian Ethic?" (January 25, 1929), in *TF*, 345-51.

"It is the problem of concretization in proclamation that presently concerns me so. It is simply not enough and therefore wrong to say that only the Holy Spirit can be the principle of concretization."

But why did Bonhoeffer set his requirements so high, if he could avoid them by not attaching such claims to Christian ethics? If in homiletics it is a precarious matter to identify the Word of God with human words, how much more so in politics. But Bonhoeffer wanted both and drew an analogy between the two for the sake of the prophetic character of the church. The point of comparison between preaching and ethics he found in the concept of "sacrament." Before Sutz he asks, "The concretization of the proclamation of grace is the sacrament. What is then the sacrament of the ethical, of the commandment?" (*GS*, 1:34). Bonhoeffer returned to that question in 1932 in his summer lectures, "Does a Christian Ethics Exist?" (*GS*, 5:275-300), and also in the address that he delivered on July 26, 1932, as youth secretary of the World Alliance for Promoting International Friendship through the Churches, "On the Theological Basis of the Work of the World Alliance" (*TF*, 96-101; *NRS*, 157-73). The high requirements that he placed on the concreteness of proclamation by the church appear to be tied to the great authority that he attributed to the church. The church, as his audience in Ciernohorské Kúpele in 1932 got to hear (and as one already knew from *Communion of Saints*), is *Christus praesens,* the presence of Christ on earth. The word of the church is the word of the present Christ; it is gospel and commandment. After that introduction, which loaded the responsibility of the ecumenical movement a lot higher than some of his audience wanted, Bonhoeffer continued, "Because of the *Christus praesens,* the word of the church here and now must be a valid, binding word" (*TF*, 98).

Remarkable in this context is that Bonhoeffer did not legitimate the authority with which the church speaks by an appeal to the authority of God, but let it depend on the adequacy with which it evaluates the situation. That is the only way that the word can become flesh. "Someone can only speak to me with authority if a word from the deepest knowledge of my humanity encounters me here and now in all my reality. Any other word is impotent. The word of the church to the world must therefore encounter the world in all its present reality from the deepest knowledge of the world, if it is to be authoritative. The church must be able to say the Word of God, the word of authority, here and now, in the most concrete way possible, from knowledge of the situation. The church may not therefore preach timeless principles, however true, but only commandments which are true today. God is 'always' God to us 'today'" (*TF*, 98). The promise becomes concrete for the hearer, but the commandment must already be concrete on the tongue of the proclaimer. The incarnation of the Word begins for Bonhoeffer in the analysis that the speaker makes of the concrete situation. Bonhoeffer concisely summarizes his views in this context by introducing the concept of sacrament. "What the sacrament is for the preaching of the Gospel, the knowledge of firm reality is for the preaching of the sacrament. *Reality is the sacrament of command*" (*NRS*, 164).[23]

One can say that this is asking for trouble. Whoever sets the stakes that high with the church as *Christus praesens* will not get the whole church to play its role. Bonhoeffer was to experience that in the ecumenical movement. But even if he had succeeded, he would never get the church to speak of one accord. Should one disarm or rearm? To Bonhoeffer's great sorrow the ecumenical movement had no clear answer in the 1930s, and for many the pacifism that he defended with an appeal to the Sermon on the Mount was unacceptable. Bonhoeffer foresaw the problem. One can label the "solution" that he suggested as "typically Bonhoeffer," but that does not make it less dissatisfying. "We can look at the difficulty squarely and then despite all the dangers we can venture to do something *either* by keeping a qualified and intentional silence of ignorance *or* by daring to put the commandment, definitely, exclusively and radically" (*NRS*, 163).

One could call that a "qualified silence," a silence for the sake of the word, significant in its pregnancy. But we cannot avoid the impression that an outside hearer would interpret it as a form of embarrassment. The singular clarity that Bonhoeffer later attributed to the voice and call of Jesus, so that one followed directly without any reflection, seems to be more of a theological construction on the basis of an ideal than a viable objective for church and ecumenical action. The term "qualified silence" makes an ethical virtue of theological necessity (i.e., embarrassment), and that is more than it deserves. The radical direction that Bonhoeffer lent to his theology of the Word clearly encounters its limits here.[24] It binds speaking by the

---

23. Cf. *GS*, 5:299 ("Does a Christian Ethics Exist?" 1932).

24. Bonhoeffer continued to defend this viewpoint, as in his *Ethics*: "If God's commandment is not clear, definite, and concrete to the last detail, then it is not God's commandment" (*E*, 245).

church to conditions under which it threatens to succumb before anything is ever said.

5.8 The Credibility of the Church

In that connection Bonhoeffer added another condition that increasingly frustrated him, because the church could not answer up to it. Here again the issue is ethical. A speaker who wants his word to count as God's Word must be credible.

One can say that Bonhoeffer's *Cost of Discipleship* is one great summons to the church to make its actions suit its words or, as he put it, to let the cheap grace of the churches become again God's costly grace. Grace is to be understood not as a principle, an idea, or a system, but as a living Word, the re-creation of one's existence (*CD*, 52). That word comes to us as a call to follow that requires direct obedience. The radicalness of the book lies not only in the inescapable act of hearing that Word that allows no compromise ("God's language is clear enough," *CD*, 188), but also in the fact that the hearers of the Word become, as followers of Christ, bearers of the Word. "They are now Christ's fellow-workers, and will be like him in all things. Thus they are to meet those to whom they are sent as if they were Christ himself. When they are welcomed into a house, Christ enters with them. They are bearers of his presence" (*CD*, 197). That requires self-sacrifice. The homiletics that Bonhoeffer develops in those same years cannot manage without a radical ethics of discipleship.

That is the direct consequence of the fact that Bonhoeffer attributes such a performative power to the Word of God. The Word has to effectuate its own reality, that is, create a community of followers as a concrete form of salvation. In the lectures on homiletics Bonhoeffer offers a description of the truth of the gospel. I already referred to the passage (5.2), but I am now interested in how it continues. "This truth is not the result of deductions; it is not the communication of a certain body of doctrine. It is truth that has taken place. It creates its own form of existence. It is possible for the church to preach pure doctrine that is nonetheless untrue. The truthfulness of it hinges upon the form of manifestation which the church adopts for itself. This form, however, implies discipleship" (*WP*, 139). Bonhoeffer would continually (as later in prison) and indissolubly connect proclamation and the social form of the church, a condition under which he had seen his church succumb.[25] In his lectures on homiletics that requirement is a constitutive element of the theory of proclamation. "To the preached word belongs the acting of the church. . . . Word and deed were a unity in the life of Christ. We have to be witnesses to this unity. But there occurs a falsification of the testimony if we think we have to add something to this witness through our experience" (*WP*, 132).

Just as Bonhoeffer's homiletics drew in its wake a radical ethics, so did his biblical hermeneutic require an obedient following. There too we encounter the same condition that he placed on effective speaking of God, the credibility of the speaker. In his address on "The Contemporary Interpretation [*Vergegenwärtigung*] of the New Testament" (1935; *NRS*, 308-25),[26] Bonhoeffer asserts that the biblical text does not have to justify itself in the present age but that the present age must justify itself before the biblical message. I will not deal with this hermeneutics further at this point, nor with the question whether it is tenable. I only point to the conclusion of the lecture, which was held before an audience of ministers of the Confessing Church. It has been preserved only in the form of a few random notes. Bonhoeffer speaks concretely of the persecution of the Jews and mentions Proverbs 31:8, "Open your mouth for the voiceless" (see 2.3). To answer the question whether a real presence of the biblical text is possible, he points not to methods of exegesis but to the actions of the church. "Here the decision will really be made whether we are still the church of the present Christ," states Bonhoeffer, and then clearly names the Jewish question (*NRS*, 325). He concludes his address with the following proposition.

> The decisive freedom for the presentation of the New Testament message consists in making it credible. The world's real offence at the church's proclamation no longer lies in the incomprehensibility of its texts and sayings about the cross and resurrection, but in their credibility. Because the church and its pastors say something different from what they do; because there is no difference between the life of a pastor and the life of a citizen. Now the way of life of the preacher is the medium of presentation [*Vergegenwärtigung*]. And presentation means "to

25. Cf. Ebeling, "The 'Non-religious Interpretation of Biblical Concepts,'" 122n.4, on the "inseparable association of the proclamation and form of the church" in *LPP*, though Ebeling loses view of the latter. Cf. chap. 1, n.19.

26. See also *TF*, 149-52.

make credible" so far as in us lies. Thus the question remains under this theme — how far we have already made the words of the text incredible by our life and by the life of the church. (*NRS*, 325)

The last sentence makes clear that in this respect Bonhoeffer was deeply disappointed in his expectations. His disillusionment on the total failure of the Confessing Church with respect to the persecution of the Jews became even greater in the late 1930s. In the letters from prison, as I have already pointed out, he expressed his disappointment in the form of a firm critique of the church. In the baptismal sermon Bonhoeffer held the church directly responsible for the fact that the liberating Word of God had become powerless. The bond between the Word of God and proclamation by the church, which was so ingrained in Bonhoeffer's theological scheme of the 1930s, was severely tested to the breaking point.

6 The Aristocratic Word

Resistance and Imprisonment

Did the Bonhoeffer who was arrested on April 5, 1943, defend the same theology of the Word as in Barcelona and Finkenwalde? If so, did he keep doing so during the emotional trials that awaited him in two years of imprisonment? If he were asked, he would answer positively. After a year in his prison cell he wrote to Bethge, "I've certainly learnt a great deal, but I don't think that I have changed very much" (*LPP*, 275; April 22, 1944). There were people who changed significantly, but he did not think that he belonged to that category. "Neither of us has really had a break in our lives," was Bonhoeffer's judgment. "I sometimes used to long for something of the kind, but today I think differently about it. Continuity with one's own past is a great gift, too."

In the first sentence quoted he was probably referring to the period in which he wrote *Cost of Discipleship*, the book in which he called for the church to break radically with the world and for Christians to break with their biographical ties. Even though he still stood by what he wrote, he could now see the dangers of it (*LPP*, 369; July 21, 1944). The continual assault that imprisonment perpetrated on his identity did not permit any destabilizing experiments with his own personality. Bonhoeffer had to go all out just to keep his head above water. Only then would he succeed in remaining "himself." The continuity indicated is a continuity for which he had fought. This is not an objective fact but a subjective assessment. It sounds like, "I have made it thus far," as a triumph over the attempts to break him that had been going on for more than a year. To say, "I have not experienced a break," is in that context the same as saying, "I have not yet been broken." For that reason Bonhoeffer can declare continuity with the past as "a great gift."

One must not infer too much from Bonhoeffer's own assessments of discontinuity and development in his life. They were part of a strategy for mental survival. The conclusion that the theologian Bonhoeffer remained unchanged is therefore premature. In the same letter to Bethge Bonhoeffer speaks of the "hardships" that in the course of time can make one insensitive. It is apparent that the past year had not been easy for him. The spiritual "trials" *(Anfechtung)* one finds in Luther's theology had become daily reality for him. Once they are over, Bonhoeffer admits, the world will look quite different than before. He does not speak, however, of insensitiveness (which could have occurred, but which he has fortunately been spared), but of clarification, which brings him to the insight, "I now see the same things quite differently." Does that also hold for his views on speaking about God? One hears Bonhoeffer adhering to the same theology of the Word as he has always done, but one can say that in several respects it has been clarified, refined. It has been reduced to its essence and has lost all the trimmings. The letter in which Bonhoeffer assesses a year of imprisonment precedes by only a week the letter in which he for the first time introduces the notions of "a world come of age" and the "non-religious Christianity," concepts that he had never employed in his theology, at least never with such intensity (*LPP*, 279-80; April 30, 1944). If the theology that Bonhoeffer produced in prison is characterized by a great deal of continuity, then it is likewise also capable of integrating a new horizon of experience. The concept of the Word of God is reflected on in a new "worldly" context and loses its self-evidence in the context of the church.

6.1 The "Declericalization" of Proclamation

That process of deepening and secularization, of progression and development, can be illustrated by a look at the "Thoughts on the Day of the Baptism," a text that Bonhoeffer composed about the same time as the letters on "non-religious interpretation" (May 1944) and that I analyzed in chapter two. In this baptismal sermon the constants of Bonhoeffer's theology of the Word can be found: (1) the presupposition of a God who speaks; (2) the characteristic creative and transforming power of the Word; (3) waiting and silence as the proper posture toward the Word; and (4) the church as a place where the Word is proclaimed and witnessed to, a calling that it does not satisfy (see 2.2). Those are the elements of continuity, which undergo an unprecedented radicalization in the baptismal sermon but which are not surrendered.

A new element in Bonhoeffer's concept of the Word of God might be indicated by the fact that he speaks of the Word as a "new language" and qualifies it as being "perhaps quite non-religious." Insights are introduced that Bonhoeffer gropingly attempted to describe and whose consequences he sought to think through during his imprisonment. How should we interpret this situation? Is it a breaking point in Bonhoeffer's theology or a new accent? Insight into the new horizon of experience with which he had been confronted since 1940 can help to clarify the issue.

From the time of Finkenwalde and the lectures on homiletics a lot happened to Bonhoeffer. The Gestapo had already closed the seminary of the Confessing Church in October of 1937. He continued that work for a time in a kind of diaspora until the Nazis made that impossible as well. In 1939 Bonhoeffer had a chance to elude the impending war and seek refuge in the United States. But after a few decisive weeks, in July of 1939 he returned with the resolve, as he later formulated it in prison, to stay "involved in Germany's fate." He became more and more actively involved in the political and military resistance to Hitler from 1941 on. His international contacts in the ecumenical movement functioned as a cover for exchanging information on resistance activities with the Allies. Bonhoeffer traveled several times to Sweden and Switzerland, officially commissioned by counterintelligence, but in fact at the service of the resistance movement. He led a double life of a minister who used his office as a cover for taking part in a coup d'état.

His solidarity with the Confessing Church had not decreased in the meantime, but the relationship had become less intimate. He still considered it to be *his* church, but he had become more convinced of its great failings. In mid-1941 he wrote a "confession of guilt" as part of his *Ethics*. There he stated that the church "was silent when it should have cried out because the blood of the innocent was crying aloud to heaven. It has failed to speak the right word in the right way and at the right time" (*E*, 92). He could hardly have more strikingly formulated the expectation he had of proclamation by the church of the Word of God, but also how the church had failed to live up to that expectation. Bonhoeffer demanded that the church confess that it had been a witness to violence and murder perpetrated on "countless innocent people" without raising its voice. "It is guilty of the deaths of the weakest and most defenceless brothers of Jesus Christ" (*E*, 93). The church appears, therefore, to be the weakest link in Bonhoeffer's doctrine of the four "forms" of the Word. God speaks clear language, but the Word has been smothered by the silence of the church. That is true not only for ethics but also for a theology that does not sufficiently take into account the changing historical and cultural context. In the letter from prison that accompanied the "Outline for a Book" that Bonhoeffer sent to Bethge on August 3, 1944, we read, "The church must come out of its stagnation. We must move out again into the open air of intellectual discussion with the world, and risk saying controversial things, if *we* are to get down to the serious problems of life" (*LPP*, 378, emphasis mine).

That last *we* is quite telling. The Confessing Church is still *his* church, and Bonhoeffer, even from prison, kept expecting a lot of it. He did not tone down his high-strung ecclesiology, now that he had noticed that the church had not lived up to it. On the contrary, he increased its intensity. "The church is the church only when it exists for others" (*LPP*, 382). That was his wish for the church that would soon have to be erected in a new Europe on the ruins left behind. The specific ideas that he had for the church (dispensing of its property, ministers engaged in secular work to support themselves, etc.) I have already indicated (2.5). He must have had those things in mind when, in the baptismal sermon, he spoke of the "melting-pot" with regard to the form of the church (*LPP*, 300). But the church as it was could in no way fulfill its mission. Bonhoeffer increased his distance from the church by emphasizing that failure.

He also distanced himself from the empirical church theologically. No one should seek shelter behind the faith of the church, he argued. "To say that it is the church's business, not mine, may be a clerical evasion, and outsiders always regard it as such" (*LPP*, 382). In his plans for the postwar church, Bonhoeffer directed special attention to the training for the ministry and the manner in which that ministry was to be practiced (*LPP*, 383). The credibility of the church had been severely violated, not in the least by its official representatives. The preacher Bonhoeffer felt obligated to come down from the pulpit (see 5.5). In his being a Christian he no longer felt supported by the institution of the church, nor did he want that support. His speaking about God had become unprotected, no longer legitimized by any homiletic or pastoral context.

During his participation in the resistance and his imprisonment he simultaneously distanced himself from the church and drew nearer to the world. Through his resistance activities Bonhoeffer associated more and more with persons who had only distant ties to the church. Again he breathed the atmosphere of his upper-middle-class environment among people who, like his own family, no longer wanted to attend church because of the "pious chatter" (see 3.5). That did not leave Bonhoeffer's theology unaffected. In a letter to Bethge from June 25, 1942, written on the train to Munich, Bonhoeffer stated, "My recent activity, which has been predominantly in the secular sphere, keeps making me think" (*TF*, 499). Finkenwalde seemed far away, where in 1936 he wrote to his students: "No day of our life in office may go past without our having read the Bible on it" (*TF*, 436).

In the letter of June 25, 1942, Bonhoeffer observed that in his own spiritual practice he had not lived up to what he had written in his books. He let that be for what it was, without getting a bad conscience from it or seeking to resist it, although he recognized that "spiritually" he "has had much richer times." On the other hand he wanted to learn some theology from his "secular activity." He did so by setting accents in his thought that would only become stronger in prison. "I detect that a rebellion against all things 'religious' is growing in me. Often it amounts to an instinctive horror" (*TF*, 499). He hardly excused himself for that antipathy, but went on to offer a sort of justification, in which he made clear that his increasing antireligiousness was not at the expense of his faith. "I'm not religious by nature. But I have to think continually of God and Christ; authenticity, life, freedom and mercy mean a great deal to me. It is just their religious manifestations that are so unattractive. Do you understand?" Bonhoeffer added that as far as he was concerned, such insights were not new. But he wanted to let them grow and ripen. "Since I feel a knot is about to explode within me here, I'm letting these things have their head and not resisting them. That's the way in which I understand my present activity in the secular sphere" (*TF*, 499).

It was apparently acceptable for Bonhoeffer to allow his theology to be influenced by the new "secular" situation in which he found himself. A word is only "true," he would write a short time later from prison, if it is specifically cut to fit the situation in which it is spoken. For him, that held also for the Word of God, which seeks to become incarnate in every new situation.

In a brief essay on what it means to speak the truth, Bonhoeffer dealt with the moral question, whether under all circumstances one has to tell the truth. The question is understandable in a situation of daily interrogations and the constant danger of betrayal. The essay, however, not only addresses the question directly but also indicates how important Bonhoeffer considered the "pragmatic context" (see 2.3) for speaking. A different context requires different words and lends a different face to truth.

The truth of a word depends not only on what is said, but also on how, by whom and to whom, and at what moment. "The truthful word is not in itself constant; it is as much alive as life itself. . . . Every utterance or word lives and has its home in a particular environment. The word in the family is different from the word in business or in public. The word that has come to life in the warmth of a personal relationship is frozen to death in the cold air of public existence. . . . Each word must have its own place and keep to it" (E, 328-29). At the end of the essay, in what we could call a small "speech-act theory," Bonhoeffer summarizes the conditions that "truthful" speaking has to satisfy.

> How can I speak the truth?
> 1. By perceiving who causes me to speak and what entitles me to speak.
> 2. By perceiving the place at which I stand.
> 3. By relating to this context the object about which I am making some assertion.
>
> It is tacitly assumed in these rules that all speech is subject to certain conditions; . . . it has its place, its time and its task, and consequently also its limits. . . .
>
> Anyone who speaks without a right and a cause to do so is an idle chatterer. . . .
>
> An utterance without reference is empty. It contains no truth. (E, 333)[1]

Whoever recognizes and subscribes to the "laws of speech" (see 5.3) in that manner would also want to test speaking about God by them. Even if the "object" (the gospel) is the same, Bonhoeffer would have to reckon with the place (resistance, prison) of the conversation partners ("world come of age," "non-religious people," "Nazi interrogators"), those for and to whom

---

1. "What Is Meant by 'Telling the Truth'?" (E, 326-34).

one speaks. He would also have to take into account the waning authority of the Confessing Church, which legitimizes one's speaking about God. Those who want to speak the Word of God can no longer seek the support of the office of ministry, but must speak of their own accord.

It becomes apparent that Bonhoeffer was willing to accept that awareness of the context in all of its consequences. Prison drove him even more strongly to attempt to speak about God outside the standard language of the church. For his was a church that had little feeling for the historical and cultural context in which it spoke its Word.[2] The people Bonhoeffer met in prison were different from the people with whom he had dealt in the resistance movement. Whereas in the resistance he had primarily met people of the upper middle class with little or no connections with the church, in Tegel he was confronted with "religionless working people and many other kinds of people" (*LPP,* 280). However different, both horizons of experience are comparable in a sense. They both drive him to the same *declericalization* of the proclamation of the Word. Bonhoeffer had undoubtedly in view the secular relevance of the gospel, as an important task for church and theology when he expressed the desire for a "non-religious interpretation of the biblical concepts."

I have already observed that one must see this program as not having yet been carried out, even so far as Bonhoeffer was concerned. On June 8, 1944, he wrote: "But it's all very much in the early stages, and, as usual, I'm being led on more by an instinctive feeling for questions that will arise later than by any conclusions that I've already reached about them" (*LPP,* 325). On July 16, 1944, he continued, "The job is too big for me to finish just yet" (*LPP,* 359; see 2.4). The question is whether the dereligionization project could ever be carried out. For one thing, it is not at all clear what Bonhoeffer meant by "non-religious" in this context. In the biography, in a clarifying excursion, Bethge has summed up the various meanings that Bonhoeffer attributes to religion in his letters. He arrives at six aspects that have in common only that they are to be judged negatively in the light of a proper understanding of Christian faith. In the letters "religion" is for

2. Cf. *GS,* 5:231ff. ("The Nature of the Church," 1932; cf. also *TF,* 82-87), where Bonhoeffer accuses the church of lacking a place. "It wants to be everywhere and is, therefore, nowhere" (*TF,* 83). Lack of context is for Bonhoeffer synonymous with "religiosity" and a lack of "worldliness." "What is the proper place of the church in Christianity? The entire daily reality of the world and not any one single aspect, even if it be the ethical or religious. . . . Its word must seek the sphere of daily life" (*TF,* 85).

Bonhoeffer synonymous with (1) metaphysics (the construction of a transcendent double world), while the gospel, on the contrary, is concerned with this world. Religion focuses on (2) the salvation of the individual soul and deals only with (3) the segment of one's inner life and inner space (which Bethge calls "partiality"). The gospel, on the contrary, is also concerned with the salvation of the social community and affects all areas of life. Further, religion sees God (4) as a deus ex machina, a stopgap and hypothesis to compensate for human weakness and to offer otherwordly solutions to life's problems. The gospel, however, addresses human beings in their strength. It wants to take shape in the midst of life and not on the boundaries. Religion always seeks to acquire (5) a privileged position in society. Whoever lives according to the gospel seeks the rejected and does not go for a privileged status. Finally, religion keeps people, in Bonhoeffer's view, (6) unemancipated. It does not appeal to people's sense of responsibility, like the gospel, but robs them of it.[3]

It becomes clear from this summary how little the word "religion" denotes a specific concept in the prison letters. It is a variegated notion with cultural, historical, philosophical, and ethical aspects, both descriptive and normative. Bonhoeffer's intent does not lie in the field of religious science; instead he uses the term as a negative contrast by which he can clarify the proper understanding of Christian faith. It is more a term for internal theological usage, for distinguishing between good and bad forms of Christian faith. In 1955, before the secularization theology had exalted Bonhoeffer as its prophet, Gerhard Ebeling was correct in saying, "It is of course a formulation for the sake of theological reflection on proclamation, not a slogan to be introduced into the vocabulary of proclamation itself."[4] The term "non-religious" belongs not in the pulpit but in the preparation and evaluation of the proclamation at home. It is a sort of meta-criterion, by which speaking about God is to be measured, not part of that speaking. That is the only way we can understand the comment on a "new language" that is "perhaps totally non-religious." Bonhoeffer binds proclamation to a number of conditions that became more and more important for him in the experiences of resistance and imprisonment. The Word will

3. Bethge, *Dietrich Bonhoeffer,* 774-82.
4. Ebeling, "The 'Non-religious Interpretation of Biblical Concepts,'" 99n.1. Ebeling describes the basic structure of Bonhoeffer's concept of religion as "the supplementing of reality by God." The concept of "religionlessness" is "coping with reality without God" (ibid., 148, 150).

only sound redeeming and liberating if the proclamation of it (1) is not an escape from this world; (2) reaches further than the inner life of individuals; (3) does not take God to be a stopgap *(Lückenbüsser)*; (4) addresses people's responsibility; and (5) does not cater to the powerful or to those with clerical status.

When, however, Bonhoeffer makes a factual observation in his letters that we are entering a "religionless" era and that people "as they are" can no longer be religious (*LPP*, 279), he then uses the concept of religion in a totally different sense. He employs it in a descriptive, nonnormative sense, which can be tested with regard to its truth. Religion is, then, "a historically conditioned and transient form of human self-expression" (*LPP*, 173) and has suddenly become a cultural-historical category. In that case one has to observe that Bonhoeffer was apparently mistaken or has yet to be proved correct. The escape from reality, the critical center of his concept of religion, is still just as popular as in his time, even if it seeks other forms than those of traditional Christianity. If that is "religion," an escape from reality with God as an alibi, then religion is still thriving today in the West. Coming of age, worldly and religionless, is what people should be. After centuries of a process of rationalization and modernization they have no reason not to be. In this, Bonhoeffer is correct, but it has not yet happened.

One has to conclude that Bonhoeffer's usage of the concept of religion, on the one hand descriptive (that's the way people are) and on the other hand normative (that's the way people should be), is confusing and frustrates his own program of a "non-religious" interpretation. But I cannot look into the question of Bonhoeffer and religion further at this point. I only note that the primary intent of Bonhoeffer's usage of the term "non-religious" is to place a number of restrictive criteria upon the church's speaking about God. If the proclamation of God's Word is to be truly liberating and redeeming, then it will have to help people to live in this reality and not allow or even invite them to try to escape from it. That is no new insight for Bonhoeffer, for his aversion to "religion" and his emphasis on "responsibility" can be traced to his early writings. Bonhoeffer read Nietzsche avidly, long before his imprisonment, and shared Nietzsche's views on human weakness being caused by religion and on strong human beings come of age not needing religion. But the emphasis on the "worldly" character of the gospel, reinforced by his disappointment in the church and by his experiences in resistance and imprisonment, finally became so great that it began to dominate Bonhoeffer's thought. That Bonhoeffer no longer could or wanted to limit speaking about God to the context of the church, but thought it also possible even outside the church or especially outside the church, contributed to a great extent to that shift in accent.

The subsequent declericalization that his theology of the Word underwent does not signify in my opinion a fundamental break with his previous theology, but a development within it, whereby Bonhoeffer attempted to integrate a new horizon of experience into his views on speaking about God.[5] The tension was driven to great heights. The hearer of the Word and the historical and cultural context in which the hearer lives are more than ever granted a say. And the authority of the one who speaks the Word can no longer be assumed to come from the church. Can the church still proclaim the Word, now that people see that it does not always embody that Word? Or does the Word take on new forms? In the letters this issue of ecclesiology remains, as Bethge has commented, an unsolved question.[6]

6.2 "There Is Too Much Talk" (The Impotence and Misuse of Words)

In Tegel one encounters the same Bonhoeffer, careful in his speech, cautious in his treatment of common words, in awe of the great Word. His prison experiences confirmed his intuitions more than contradicted them. It is impressive to see how he again and again succeeded in turning the trials of imprisonment into an enriching learning process for himself.[7] "I'm often finding the world nauseating and burdensome," is a confession that he let slip out only once to Bethge (*LPP*, 162). Whatever tortures of heat, cold, hunger, illness, humiliation, hope, and despair lie behind that, he did not tell about them openly, and we can only suspect things by reading between the lines. He did speak openly on his observations and experiences and about the fact that he found himself "led back quite simply to prayer

5. Cf. Mayer and Zimmerling, *Mensch hinter Mauern*, 135: "In the reception of Bonhoeffer until now too much has been said about the enigma of the nonreligious interpretation, and too little attention has been paid to how far Bonhoeffer carried it through in the letters and papers from prison."

6. Bethge, *Dietrich Bonhoeffer*, 790-91 ("An Unfinished Ecclesiology").

7. Cf. C. Gremmels and H. Pfeiffer, *Theologie und Biographie: Zum Beispiel Dietrich Bonhoeffer* (Theology and biography: For example, Dietrich Bonhoeffer) (Munich: Chr. Kaiser, 1983). See also de Lange, *Grond onder de voeten*, 272ff.

and the Bible," and in that respect his "time of imprisonment is being a very wholesome though drastic cure" (*LPP*, 149). In all of this Bonhoeffer remained the theologian of the Word and the believing Christian in and through an unwavering trust in God. In order to survive, he again took up the pious practices that he had learned in the 1930s. Prayer, church hymns (especially those of Paul Gerhardt), reading the Bible, the daily texts *(Losungen)* for meditation of the Moravian Brethren, the liturgical year, rituals like making the sign of the cross, these all lent structure to Bonhoeffer's daily life at a time that chaos threatened it.[8]

Practicing the art of conversation, in which he had been brought up, was something that with only rare exceptions he could forget about in prison.[9] Conversations there were governed by distrust. Shortly before his imprisonment Bonhoeffer complained that he and his fellow resisters had by necessity learned "the arts of equivocation and pretence; experience has made us suspicious of others and kept us from being truthful and open" ("After Ten Years," *LPP*, 16). That situation only became worse in the innumerable interrogations to which he was subjected. The very limited leave that he was granted to speak with his fiancée, his friend Bethge, or members of his family was in no way a compensation. Under great tension and the supervision of a guard, one can never say what one wants to say. But is it ever possible to say that in words? After a visit from Maria von Wedemeyer he wrote his parents: "What one can say at such a time is so trivial, but that's not the main thing" (*LPP*, 71-72). He could only have nodded in agreement when he saw the letter of his brother-in-law, Hans von Dohnanyi, who was arrested on the same day and who wrote Bonhoeffer about the visit of his wife Christel. "What can one say in the presence of other people? How immeasurably difficult, impossible it is to open one's heart" (*LPP*, 24; April 23, 1943).[10] The ability to discern what remained unsaid in the words of another had to be fully activated now (3.4).

---

8. "It is no longer possible to assert a break in Bonhoeffer's theology and spirituality during the years in prison" (Mayer and Zimmerling, *Mensch hinter Mauern*, 10). For a summary of all facets of Bonhoeffer's impressive praxis of faith in prison, see ibid., 37-38.

9. With the subaltern Linke Bonhoeffer seems to have carried on good conversations, even if Bonhoeffer was the superior partner. There is a degree of pride in his observation that "this sort of conversation is a new world to him, and I myself believe that quite objectively it is something unique" (*LPP*, 315).

10. Cf. *LPP*, 202 (February 1, 1944): "The visits are very different from each other, although of course I enjoy each one of them."

To his parents Bonhoeffer sighs after a month and a half about his literary experiences with Stifter and Gotthelf: "If only we could talk to each other about these things. For all my sympathy with the contemplative life, I am not a born Trappist. Nevertheless, a period of enforced silence may be a good thing" (*LPP*, 40). The connection he then makes between meditation and the interpretation of Scripture, with reference to Catholic monastic orders, is not new to us, given his earlier book, *Life Together* (see 5.4). But such piety, he admits, is too much for him now. Silence is not always fruitful. "When shall we be able to talk together again, for hours at a time?" (*LPP*, 220). "When shall we be able to talk together again?" (*LPP*, 232). "It would be fine to have a word from you about all this" (*LPP*, 282). These are sentences from Bonhoeffer's letters to Bethge in which he yearns for a good conversation with the man with whom he has shared all of his theological insights and discoveries for years. The correspondence with his friend, which thanks to the assistance of a sympathetic guard was possible from the end of 1943 until his transfer to the Gestapo prison, soon took on the form of a dialogue, which gradually restored Bonhoeffer's stagnating theological creativity (*LPP*, 160; December 15, 1943).[11]

The experience of the deficit of the spoken word was, however, compensated, at times amply, by other means of communication. After praising the tireless faithfulness of his parents, Bonhoeffer writes: "There are situations in which the simplest action is more than the greatest outlines and plans and discussions" (*LPP*, 232-33). That faithfulness expresses itself in their visits, but even more in small things they leave behind for the prisoner. Fruit preserves, cookies, tobacco, cigarettes and cigars, wine, grapes, baked rabbit, cocoa, eggs, a warm fur, but also bunches of dahlias, blossoming fall flowers, a watch of the fallen father of Maria von Wedemeyer, a Christmas cup from Dietrich's grandfather, candles, photographs of members of the family, and other familiar items all pass the threshold of Bonhoeffer's cell in the two years of imprisonment.[12] These were practical and nourishing, but at the same time they were a sign of endearment and

11. "It's really quite wonderful that the dialogue remains intact, and I feel that it's always the most fruitful that I have" (March 24, 1944, *LPP*, 236) Cf. C. Gremmels, in Gremmels and Huber, *Theologie und Freundschaft*, 135-53.

12. Even though Dietrich Bonhoeffer also had poor and too little food in prison (cf. "Report on Prison Life," *LPP*, 250), in comparison with some other members of the family, he was not as bad off as they (Karl-Friedrich Bonhoeffer, in his "Memories of a Survivor," *LPP*, 409-10).

nearness. "Material things become the vehicles of spiritual realities. I think this is analogous to the need felt in all religions for the visible appearance of the Spirit in the sacrament" (*LPP*, 55).[13] Had Bonhoeffer not once characterized the reality of the ethical act as the sacrament of the Word (5.7)? "The mere fact that you have been near me, the tangible evidence that you are still thinking and caring about me," is the response of Bonhoeffer to the package that his parents delivered for him shortly after his arrest (*LPP*, 26; April 25, 1943). On November 26, 1943, a cigar that had made a long trip from Switzerland in Bethge's baggage and that turned out to be from Karl Barth was delivered to him. It was as though it meant more to Bonhoeffer than a thick volume of Barth's dogmatics. "Karl's cigar is on the table in front of me, and that is something really indescribable" (*LPP*, 145). Ordinary things could thus become signs that speak a clearer language than words ever could.

In the years of resistance and imprisonment his insight into the impotence and misuse of words was sharpened. Bonhoeffer's appreciation of the *quality* of words became stronger, hence his complaint in the letter of April 11, 1944, that "aimless gossip gets on my nerves terribly" (*LPP*, 271).

It could be, however, that Bonhoeffer had not lowered his standards but that, in his surroundings, words assumed less and less importance. By that he does not refer only to the volleys of abuse and the shouting to which he was exposed in prison ("Report on Prison Life," *LPP*, 252; cf. 254). In his *Ethics* Bonhoeffer had already commented that National Socialism infiltrated not only the world but the people's language as well. In the list of values that "the void engulfs," Bonhoeffer includes not only life, history, family, nation, and faith, but also language (*E*, 85). Elsewhere he mentions how great humanistic values like reason, education, tolerance, justice, and self-determination were undermined by Nazism, while others, like nation and society, were being perverted and turned into slogans of propaganda (*E*, 38). Germany's good name was being dragged through the slime of an evil ideology, while the Nazi announcement of "great times" only called forth more suffering and misery (*FP*, 119). The Nazi government, however, kept up its pathetic speaking about the "sanctity of life," the "majesty of death," the "majesty of the nation," and "service to the nation." Great words were thus perverted, misused, made suspect, or "stolen"

---

13. To Maria von Wedemeyer he wrote, "Everything 'material' you send me here, transforms itself at mealtimes into tokens of your solidarity and love and loyalty" (*LL*, 120).

(*E*, 55).[14] "The small band of the upright is reviled. Their bravery is insubordination; their self-control is called pharisaism; their independence, arbitrariness; and their masterfulness, arrogance" (*E*, 73). The concepts that had once constituted the moral code of middle-class society were turned into their opposite and appeared impotent in the face of the power that misused them (cf. "After Ten Years," *LPP*, 3ff.).

In prison Bonhoeffer sought an antidote to that assault on language. He found it in the literature of the nineteenth century. Especially in the writings of Jeremias Gotthelf and Adalbert Stifter he came across a "purity of language" that he missed elsewhere. Like a thirsty person in the desert, he quenched his thirst with the quiet and simplicity of their writings (*LPP*, 40, 125).

In the midst of the misuse of words that he had experienced, Bonhoeffer arrived at an even greater appreciation of silence. Hence in the drama fragment from Tegel he has Christoph say, "I am speaking to you to protect from misuse the great words given to humankind." That sentence is the beginning of a passage that Bonhoeffer rewrote three times, a sign that he attributed great value to it. The passage continues, "They [the great words] don't belong in the mouths of the masses, or in the headlines of the newspapers, but in the hearts of the few who guard and protect them with their lives. . . . Those who are guardians of genuine values with their lives, their work and their homes turn in disgust from the ringing rhetoric that is supposed to turn the masses into prophets. Which well-meaning person can still utter the degraded words *freedom, brotherhood,* even *Germany?* He seeks them in the quietness of the sanctuary which only the humble and faithful may approach. . . . Let us honor the great values by silence for a time, let us learn to do what is just without words for a while" (*FP*, 33-34).

Again, silence for Bonhoeffer did not mean muteness; rather, it was at the service of speaking. The great political values were to be honored by it, not forgotten or disposed of, so that they could once again be uttered aloud and publicly. A plea was made for an asceticism in speaking, a silence while waiting. In the words of Christoph in the drama fragment, however diffi-

14. Cf. V. Klemperer, *LTI: Notizbuch eines Philologen* (LTI: Notebook of a philologist) (Leipzig: Reclam, 1985), 21, on the Lingua Tertii Imperii, the language of the Third Reich: "The Third Reich creatively coined a minimum number of words of its language, probably none at all."

cult it is, everything depends on doing, "without words, yes, not understood and alone if need be, . . . what is necessary and just" (*FP*, 34).

The parallel of this passage with that of the baptismal sermon in which the cause of Christians is called "quiet and hidden" is easy to see. It is not only the political but also the genuinely Christian values (and they partially coincide) that share in the decay of words. The summons to a "discipline of the secret" *(disciplina arcani)* by the church, which Bonhoeffer issues in that context, has to be understood in terms of the same dialectic of silence and speech (see 2.5). In a society in which the great words resound in the streets and are then made powerless or turned into their opposite, the same words cannot be better honored than by retiring them for a while to silence and by seeking to maintain their true meaning only in intimate settings. Whether they be political or religious values, for the time being they prosper the best, like a grain of wheat in the earth, in the inner sphere. For the church that means prayer and the place of worship (*LPP*, 281, 286). Now that the public square has been occupied by the enemy of the word, public silence becomes a way to go underground and resist.

The moratorium that Bonhoeffer advocates in the public usage of the great words is, therefore, to be seen as an act of defiance under Nazi rule. It is an act of resistance to the fascist slogan, "You are nothing. Your nation is everything." In that way every private life becomes public. No personal sphere of life is allowed that can withdraw itself from the public sphere.[15] One should read the drama fragment against the background of that context. On political values: "The great words that are given to human beings must be protected from misuse." Parallel to that is what Bonhoeffer writes on Christian values and the discipline of maintaining silence in given areas of one's life of faith. "That means that a discipline of the secret must be restored whereby the *mysteries* of Christian faith are protected against profanation" (*LPP*, 286). In both cases Bonhoeffer advocates the same temporary asceticism with regard to speech to counter the assault on words.

In his *Ethics* Bonhoeffer had formulated the insight that the meaning

---

15. Klemperer, *LTI*, 29. "The LTI has no longer a private sphere distinguishable from the public sphere, no more than it distinguishes written from spoken language. Everything is talk and everything is public. . . . You are never with yourself; never alone with your own; you always stand in the face of your nation."

and authority of words depends on the institutional context in which they are spoken. In prison he applied that insight to both the church and politics. The context of both is the "dissolution and decay" of the social and moral order (*FP*, 41; cf. *LPP*, 123). Bonhoeffer had in mind the crisis of ministry in the church (which for contemporary ears sounds progressive), but also that of upper-middle-class culture (which gives a more conservative impression) (see 2.1 and 2.3). In *Fiction from Prison* we read that marriage, family, government, and justice are no longer recognized and respected as institutions in their own right. One recalls that in the *Ethics* he developed a doctrine of the "mandates" that guaranteed their relative autonomy (*E*, 252ff.). That critique of culture can be properly interpreted only against the background of Nazism. For National Socialism there was really only one social body, only one form of life, and that was the "nation." There was only one language game, and that was the language of public propaganda.[16] The relative autonomy of the spheres of life, which in relation to each other possess a certain degree of freedom, was erased. One needs to keep that context in mind when in his essay on "speaking the truth" Bonhoeffer declares: "Each word must have its own place and keep to it. It is a consequence of the wide diffusion of the public word through the newspapers and the wireless that the essential character and the limits of the various different words are no longer clearly felt and that, for example, the special quality of the personal word is almost entirely destroyed. Genuine words are replaced by idle chatter. Words no longer possess any weight. There is too much talk. And when the limits of the various words are obliterated, when words become rootless and homeless, then the word loses truth, and then indeed there must almost inevitably be lying" (*E*, 329-30).[17] In that situation Bonhoeffer opted for a strategy of abstinence and silence.

6.3 "The Inability to Say a Christian Word to Others" (The Ultimate and the Penultimate)

Bonhoeffer applied that insight into the situatedness of words not only to political ethics but also to his theology. In his *Ethics* and *Letters and Papers*

---

16. Klemperer, *LTI*, 29.
17. "What Is Meant by 'Telling the Truth'?" (*E*, 329).

from Prison the Word that God speaks retains the same a priori that it always possessed for Bonhoeffer. In that respect there is only continuity. "It is God's own free Word, which is subject to no compulsion; for this reason it is the irreversible final word, an ultimate reality. Consequently it excludes any method of achieving it by a way of one's own" (*E*, 100-101). Faith must be related to the ultimate Word of God under all circumstances.

With ever more emphasis, however, Bonhoeffer was inclined to view human words in their relative autonomy. A human word, in its possibilities and limits, was only a penultimate word in relation to the ultimate Word of God. It was to be valued in its thorough "this-worldliness," even in view of its relation to the Word of God.

In the *Ethics* Bonhoeffer tries to integrate that insight theologically by referring to his pastoral experiences. In a letter to Erwin Sutz in 1932 he had interpreted the impotence of a pastor to say something to people during a house call as a possible failure of a pastoral care based on proclamation. In the lectures on spiritual care in Finkenwalde he had, however, allowed for a pastoral silence. In the chapter on the "ultimate and penultimate" that Bonhoeffer wrote for his *Ethics* at the end of 1940 and beginning of 1941, he was inclined to allow even more. He had made of his former pastoral neediness a theological virtue. Not knowing what to say for God's sake was not only permitted in some cases but was sometimes preferable by far to speaking.

> So that this may become quite clear, let us ask why it is that precisely in thoroughly grave situations, for instance when I am with someone who has suffered a bereavement, I often decide to adopt a "penultimate" attitude, particularly when I am dealing with Christians, remaining silent as a sign that I share in the bereaved person's helplessness in the face of such a grievous event, and not speaking the biblical words of comfort which are, in fact, known to me and available to me. Why am I often unable to open my mouth, when I ought to give expression to the ultimate? And why, instead, do I decide on an expression of thoroughly penultimate human solidarity? Is it from mistrust of the power of the ultimate word? Is it from fear of people? Or is there some positive reason for such an attitude, namely, that my knowledge of the word, my having it at my finger-tips, in other words my being, so to speak, spiritually master of the situation, bears only the appearance of the ultimate, but is in reality something entirely penultimate? Does one not in some cases, by remain-

ing deliberately in the penultimate, perhaps point all the more genuinely to the ultimate, which God will speak in God's own time (though indeed even then through a human mouth)? (*E*, 103-4)

We see that in Bonhoeffer's theology of the Word, he now lends a place in his *Ethics* to human solidarity in silence, something he had rejected in his lectures on spiritual care (5.5). Pastoral silence, he argued, is not the expression of the definitive absence of the Word, but seeks to create space for its coming. Bonhoeffer did not abandon his views on speaking about God. He still considered it possible that God comes to speak among people. But his awareness that it is an ultimate, truly last word becomes sharpened.

But one has to be willing to wait for that redeeming word. During the many night bombings that harassed the Tegel prison, Bonhoeffer noticed how difficult it was for him as a pastor to say something in the name of God. It was the aversion to exploiting religiously the weakness of others but also his care for the preciousness of the Word of God that prevented him from doing so. In a letter from January 29-30, 1944, Bonhoeffer admitted to Bethge that "I haven't so far felt able to say a Christian word to the others at such a moment. As we were again lying on the floor last night, and someone exclaimed, 'O God, O God,' (he is normally a very flippant type), I couldn't bring myself to offer him any Christian encouragement or comfort. All I did was to look at my watch and say, 'It won't last more than ten minutes now'" (*LPP*, 199). A day later Bonhoeffer returned to that experience and wrote: "I'm bad at comforting; I can listen all right, but I can hardly ever find anything to say. But perhaps the way one asks about some things and not about others helps to suggest what really matters; and it seems to me more important actually to share someone's distress than to use smooth words about it" (*LPP*, 203).

Those experiences strengthen Bonhoeffer in the conviction that religion too easily takes refuge in a cheap word and that Christian faith, properly understood, should be wary of this. He does not seem to consider himself such a bad comforter after all. He finds more and more theological reasons for his reticence to speak a Christian word. In the same letter in which he writes to Bethge, "It is only when one knows the unutterability of the name of God that one can utter the name of Jesus Christ," we also read, "One cannot and must not speak the last word before the last but one" (*LPP*, 157; see 1.1). And when the term "discipline of the secret" (*disciplina arcani*) is later introduced, it is related directly to the same distinction between the last and last but one, the ultimate and the penultimate. "What is the place of worship and prayer in a religionless situation? Does the discipline of the secret, or alternatively the difference (which I have suggested to you before) between the penultimate and the ultimate, take on a new importance here?" (*LPP,* 281; April 30, 1944). By "discipline of the secret" Bonhoeffer apparently means a silence full of significance, and by "religion" mere idle chatter.

In the same letter he speaks again of his aversion to easy, clever words. He writes that his sense of quality grows stronger, also in relation to the Word of God.

> While I'm often reluctant to mention God by name to religious people — because that name somehow seems to me here not to ring true, and I feel myself to be slightly dishonest (it's particularly bad when others start to talk in religious jargon; then I dry up almost completely and feel awkward and uncomfortable) — to people with no religion I can on occasion mention God by name quite calmly and as a matter of course. Religious people speak of God when human knowledge (perhaps simply because they are too lazy to think) has come to an end, or when human resources fail . . . I should like to speak of God not on the boundaries but at the center, not in weakness but in strength, and therefore not in death and guilt but in a person's life and goodness. As to the boundaries, it seems to me better to be silent and leave the insoluble unsolved. (*LPP,* 281-82)

Out of respect for the Word of God, Bonhoeffer stretches the distance between the penultimate and ultimate word to a maximum, without surrendering their mutual relatedness, so that there is all the room necessary for recognizing the relative impotence of human words. The redeeming word that God speaks, still through a human mouth, must remain an ultimate word that is not spoken too soon. The ultimate word will only sound credible and true if it is spoken out of solidarity in the penultimate. The Word of God is not available apart from that.

The theology of ministry and the ecclesiology that has sustained Bonhoeffer's theology up to now will, again and all the more critically, have to be revised by that insight. Only then, according to Bonhoeffer, will the church be able to regain the authority that it forfeited in the years previous. In *Ethics* Bonhoeffer speaks of the "exclusive interest in the divine mandate of proclamation" in Protestant churches, without wishing to detract from the importance of proclamation. On the contrary, in the name of proclamation he has pointed to the "failure" of the Protestant church and especially the shortcomings of its leaders in the fields of spirituality (spiritual exercises, asceticism, meditation, contemplation) as well as ethics. Bonhoeffer mentions specifically the refusal to take oaths [to Hitler] and to serve in the army (see 2.3). "This failure has necessarily detracted from the power, the abundance and the fulness of the proclamation itself, because the proclamation finds no fertile soil. In terms of parable, the commission of proclamation has been implanted in the congregation like the grain of wheat in the field; if the soil has not been prepared the seed withers away and loses its own inherent fruitfulness" (*E*, 267). The manuscript for the *Ethics* breaks off at this point. These are the last words that Bonhoeffer wrote before he was arrested on April 5, 1943.

Bonhoeffer's *Ethics* was never completed. We can now say, however, that in prison Bonhoeffer proceeded with and radicalized his thoughts on the relation between the proclamation of the church and the form in which the church is embodied. In what sense did he radicalize them? In the passage quoted from *Ethics* the image of the grain of wheat is striking. It is a dreary image. Doesn't the grain of wheat have to die before bearing fruit (John 12:24)? Apparently the depth of the church's impotence to proclaim a redeeming word, as Bonhoeffer would formulate in the baptismal sermon a year later in prison, had already been fathomed here. At the same time there is no more hopeful image than this, that for the grain that falls in fertile ground new life is a matter of dying to self and waiting attentively.

In the letters this double line of critique and hope, judgment and expectation, is continued consistently. The chasm between the word of the church and the Word of God is fathomed even more deeply. We read that too often the church has compromised itself by mixing politics with religion and has succumbed to the temptation of the cheap word. Out of respect for the divine Word Bonhoeffer refuses to resign himself to a carefree appeal to human fears and weakness. In his letter of July 8, 1944, having fully displayed his increasing sensibility to quality, he points to theologians who intimately embrace existential philosophy and psychotherapy because they so emphasize human weakness that this frailty can then be compensated for by God. "The importunity of all these people is far too unaristocratic for the Word of God to ally itself with them. The Word of God is far removed from this revolt of mistrust, this revolt from below. On the contrary, it reigns" (*LPP*, 346). It cannot be said more clearly that

Bonhoeffer's growing inability to speak about God does not arise out of fear for a deficit of human words, but out of his belief in the sovereign profusion of the Word of God.[18]

Bonhoeffer continued to hold to that a priori of the Word of God, as the baptismal sermon demonstrates. "The day will come that *people* will once more be called so to utter the word of *God* that the world will be changed and renewed by it" (*LPP*, 300, emphasis mine; see 2.2). One can now conclude that the identification of human words and the Word of God, to which Bonhoeffer as a student and in keeping with the Reformation subscribed in *Communio Sanctorum* ("praedicatio verbi divini est verbum divinum," *CS*, 160), is placed here under an almost unbearable tension without the dialectic ever being given up.

Because Bonhoeffer continued to relate human speaking (even if it assumed the form of silence) to divine speaking, there had to be a point to be found in the penultimate where they meet. It was not the pulpit, at least not to the extent that it had become a place of cheap and carefree words. The "is" in the Reformation's viewpoint on preaching, the identification of human words with the Word of God, was therefore a presence under constraints. In prison the "Word" was present for Bonhoeffer only in the attitude of *waiting*. In *Life Together* we have already seen how Bonhoeffer considered waiting for the Word to be an essential aspect of Bible meditation. In prison that waiting took on a broader significance. It is as though waiting became the expression of Bonhoeffer's entire existence. On May 16, 1944, more than a year after his arrest, without any prospect of a trial despite the innumerable interrogations, he writes to Bethge that "waiting here has become my only task" (*LPP*, 292). Bonhoeffer waited for his trial, but not just for that. He waited for the coup against Hitler to succeed. He waited for the victory of the Allies. He waited for his liberation from prison. After four months of imprisonment he writes to his parents, "This having to wait for everything is the dominating feature of my present condition" (*LPP*, 89; August 7, 1943).

Until the end Bonhoeffer succeeded in maintaining an inner vitality, despite continual disappointments, which caused him at times to confess:

18. Bonhoeffer maintains unshattered his belief in the sovereignty of God: "But all the time God still reigns in heaven" (*LPP*, 384; see 191, 276, 307, 320, 387, 393). For the relation of that waiting as a posture of faith in God's providence, see, e.g., *LPP*, 237-38, where the moment of baptism of Bethge's child is discussed: "So we can quite well wait a little and trust in God's kindly providence."

"This waiting is revolting" (*LPP,* 164). But he refused to shut himself up in the past or to be satisfied with a short-lived moment. He kept the desire and the hope for the future alive (*LPP,* 167, 271-72). Bonhoeffer remained able, thanks to an exceptional psychic resilience and an equally exceptional trust in God, to sustain the "expectation of great events" ("Who am I?" *LPP,* 348).[19]

Against the background of this ability to endure inner tensions, even if they threaten to become unbearable, the words "waiting for the redeeming Word" from the baptismal sermon take on a forceful expressiveness. Somewhere in July of 1944 Bonhoeffer jotted down on a loose piece of paper a few words in telegram style. In those notes theological reflection and the experience of imprisonment seem to intermingle.

> Why so foolish? I don't know:
> I wait and always disappointment
> I wait for God. (*LPP,* 343)

They describe not only the tension of the moment but also that of all of his theology, which is maintained until the very end. It is a theology of waiting for the redeeming Word.

It is senseless to speculate how Bonhoeffer might have developed his theology further if he had not been executed on April 9, 1945. Would he have abandoned his views on speaking about God because they proved untenable? Or would he have held them up to the church all the more forcefully as a new, challenging possibility in a period of reconstruction and recovery? We do not know with any precision. We can only conclude that from beginning to end, from Barcelona to Tegel, he continued to hold to the central intuition of Christian faith and tradition, namely, that speaking about God is possible and meaningful, because God's redeeming presence has made itself known in human language, and that, consequently, the church is called to speak that Word of God.

Bonhoeffer lived out this conviction in an honest and credible manner. Under various and difficult circumstances he attempted to express it in words. He regularly encountered its ultimate limit, that of silence. In this way he explored the possibilities and limits of human speaking about

19. Cf. *LPP,* 312-13: "To wait loyally a whole lifetime — that is to triumph over the hostility of space, i.e. separation, and over time, i.e. the past."

God and formulated the radical conditions to which such speech is bound. That is, in my opinion, Bonhoeffer's contribution to the present-day debate on religious language. He did not want to play the profusion of the Word of God off against human deficits, but wanted to honor both, without relinquishing the discovery of the Reformation that God's Word wants to be spoken through human speech.

It is perhaps more possible to be a theologian, "one who speaks about God," in a different manner. One could by definition reject the notion that God can speak to and address us and refuse to recognize the possibility that people can address each other with a word of command or promise in the name of God. The gain is great. One is safeguarded against the danger of short-circuiting human words as well as the Word of God. But the loss is just as great. One robs oneself in advance of the experience that God wants to bring the divinity to speech among people.

Bonhoeffer remained convinced until the very end that God's active presence wants to reveal itself in our speaking. That is the strong point of his theology of the Word. But this theology also has its weak side. In that context I pointed to his strong views on the Bible (5.4), his conception of a christocentric ethics (5.7), and his use of the word "religion" (2.4; 6.1).

There is one decisive link in Bonhoeffer's theological concept, however, of which one cannot say in advance whether it represents a shortcoming on the level of his theological theory or is a sign of continual failure in the everyday life of Christians. By that I mean Bonhoeffer's expectations for the church and for those who declare themselves Christian. Is their witness credible? Is it open to ordinary people as they are? Those questions remained undecided for Bonhoeffer. Perhaps that is why they still seem so relevant today on the eve of the twenty-first century.

It is Bonhoeffer's radical but unrelinquishable insight that these questions can be answered not in a theoretical manner by theologians but by the practical commitment of Christian churches. Hermeneutics is decided by ethics. In Bonhoeffer's view the best argument for the claim that the God of Jesus speaks today is the unambiguous way in which people represent God's cause in this world.

The human language in which God speaks of God is a *qualified* form of speech. It does not, like a great deal of religious language, seduce its hearers into a metaphysical escape from reality. The Word of God is most clearly understood not in a sacral space of the church but in the church's worldly obedience to its Lord. In that way, according to Bonhoeffer, the church is *Christus praesens*, Christ present in the world. Will the church in the coming century live up to this word of Bonhoeffer or betray it? It is up to the church to answer.

Bibliography

1. Writings of Dietrich Bonhoeffer

Where possible, standard English translations have been followed in the text. In other cases quotations have been translated directly from the German by the translator. The abbreviations following the editions below are used to indicate the volume quoted in the text.

1.1 German Language

Dietrich Bonhoeffer Werke. Munich: Chr. Kaiser, 1986ff. *(DBW)*.

Volume 1: *Sanctorum Communio: Eine dogmatische Untersuchung zur Soziologie der Kirche*, edited by J. von Soosten, 1986.

Volume 2: *Akt und Sein: Transzendentalphilosophie und Ontologie in der systematische Theologie*, edited by H.-R. Reuter, 1988.

Volume 3: *Schöpfung und Fall*, edited by M. Rüter and I. Tödt, 1989.

Volume 4: *Nachfolge*, edited by M. Kuske and I. Tödt, 1989.

Volume 5: *Gemeinsames Leben — Das Gebetbuch der Bibel*, edited by G. L. Müller and A. Schönherr, 1987.

Volume 6: *Ethik*, edited by I. Tödt et al., 1992.

Volume 7: *Fragmente aus Tegel*, edited by R. Bethge and I. Tödt, 1994.

Volume 9: *Jugend und Studium 1918-1927*, edited by H. Pfeifer et al., 1986.

Volume 10: *Barcelona, Berlin, Amerika 1928-1931*, edited by R. Staats et al., 1991.

Volume 11: *Ökumene, Universität, Pfarramt 1931-1932*, edited by E. Amelung and C. Strohm, 1994.

Volume 13: *London 1933-1935*, edited by H. Goedeking, M. Heimbucher, and H.-W. Schleicher, 1994.

Gesammelte Schriften, edited by E. Bethge. Munich: Chr. Kaiser, 1958ff. *(GS)*.
Volume 1: *Ökumene, 1928-1942*, 1958.
Volume 2: *Kirchenkampf und Finkenwalde, 1933-1943*, 1959.
Volume 3: *Theologie — Gemeinde, 1927-1944*, 1960.
Volume 4: *Auslegungen — Predigten, 1931-1944*, 1961.
Volume 5: *Seminare — Vorlesungen — Predigten, 1924-1941*, 1972.
Volume 6: *Tagebücher — Briefe — Dokumente, 1923-1945*, 1974.

Widerstand und Ergebung: Briefe und Aufzeichnungen aus der Haft. Neuausgabe, edited by E. Bethge. Munich: Chr. Kaiser, 1970.

1.2 English Translations

Dietrich Bonhoeffer Works. Minneapolis: Fortress Press, 1996ff.
Volume 2: *Act and Being*, edited by W. W. Floyd Jr., translated by H. M. Rumscheidt, 1996 *(AB)*.
Volume 3: *Creation and Fall: A Theological Exposition of Genesis 1–3*, edited by John W. de Gruchy, translated by Douglas Stephen Bax, 1997 *(CF)*.
Volume 5: *Life Together/Prayerbook of the Bible*, edited by G. B. Kelly, translated by D. W. Bloesch and J. H. Burtness, 1996 *(LT)*.

Christ the Center, translated by Edwin H. Robertson. New York: Harper & Row, 1978 *(CC)*.

Communion of Saints: A Dogmatic Inquiry into the Sociology of the Church, translated by Ronald Gregor Smith. New York: Harper & Row, 1963 *(CS)*.

The Cost of Discipleship, translated by R. H. Fuller and Irmgard Booth. Revised edition. New York: Macmillan, 1959 *(CD)*.

Ethics, translated by N. H. Smith. Reprint, London: SCM, 1993 *(E)*.

Fiction from Prison: Gathering up the Past, edited by Renate and Eberhard Bethge with Clifford Green, translated by Ursula Hoffmann. Philadelphia: Fortress Press, 1981 *(FP)*.

Letters and Papers from Prison, translated by R. Fuller et al. New York: Macmillan, 1972 *(LPP)*.

Love Letters from Cell 92: The Correspondence between Dietrich Bonhoeffer and Maria von Wedemeyer 1943-45, edited by Ruth-Alice von Bismarck and Ulrich Kabitz, translated by John Brownjohn. Nashville: Abingdon, 1994 *(LL)*.

No Rusty Swords: Letters, Lectures and Notes 1928-1936 from the Collected Works of Dietrich Bonhoeffer, volume 1, edited and introduced by

Edwin H. Robertson, translated by Edwin H. Robertson and John Bowden. New York: Harper & Row, 1965 *(NRS)*.

Spiritual Care, translated and with an introduction by Jay C. Rochelle. Philadelphia: Fortress Press, 1985 *(SC)*.

A Testament to Freedom: The Essential Writings of Dietrich Bonhoeffer, edited by Geffrey B. Kelly and F. Burton Nelson. Revised edition. San Francisco: HarperCollins, 1995 *(TF)*.

Bonhoeffer: Wordly Preaching (Finkenwalde Lectures on Homiletics), translated by Clyde E. Fant. Nashville/New York: Nelson, 1975 *(WP)*.

2. Other Literature

Abromeit, H.-J. *Das Geheimnis Christi: Dietrich Bonhoeffers erfahrungsbezogene Christologie* (The mystery of Christ: Dietrich Bonhoeffer's Christology as related to experience). Neukirchen: Neukirchener Verlag, 1991.

Altenähr, A. *Dietrich Bonhoeffer als Lehrer des Gebetes* (Dietrich Bonhoeffer as teacher of prayer). Würzburg: Echter, 1976.

Austin, J. L. *How to Do Things with Words.* 2d ed. Oxford: Oxford University Press, 1975.

Barth, Karl. *The Word of God and the Word of Man,* translated by Douglas Horton. Reprint, New York: Harper, 1957.

Bethge, Eberhard. *Dietrich Bonhoeffer: Man of Vision, Man of Courage,* translated by Eric Mosbacher et al., edited by Edwin Robertson. New York: Harper & Row, 1970.

———. *Am gegebenen Ort: Aufsätze und Reden, 1970-1979* (At the given place: Essays and speeches, 1970-1979). Munich: Chr. Kaiser, 1979.

———. *Zwischen Finkenwalde und Tirpitzufer: Der Ort des Gebetes in Leben und Theologie von Dietrich Bonhoeffer* (Between Finkenwalde and Tirpitzufer: The place of prayer in the life and theology of Dietrich Bonhoeffer). Kampen: Kok, 1984.

Bonhoeffer, Karl. "Lebenserinnerungen: Geschrieben für die Familie" (Memories: Written for the family), in *Karl Bonhoeffer zum Hundertsten Geburtstag am 31 März 1968* (On the occasion of Karl Bonhoeffer's centennial birthday on March 31, 1968), edited by J. Zutt et al. Berlin: Springer Verlag, 1969, 8-107.

Bulhof, I. N., and L. ten Kate, eds. *Ons ontbreken heilige namen: Negatieve theologie in de hedendaagse cultuurfilosofie* (Sacred names are lacking: Negative theology in contemporary philosophy of culture). Kampen: Kok, 1992.

Buren, Paul M. van. *The Secular Meaning of the Gospel, Based on an Analysis of Its Language.* New York: Macmillan, 1963.

Daiber, K. F. *Predigen und Hören.* Vol. 2: *Kommunikation zwischen Predigern und Hörern — Sozialwissenschaftliche Untersuchungen* (Preaching and hearing. Vol. 2: Communication between preachers and hearers — a social-scientific investigation). Munich: Chr. Kaiser, 1983.

Ebeling, Gerhard. "The 'Non-religious Interpretation of Biblical Concepts,'" in idem, *Word and Faith,* translated by James W. Leitch, 98-161. Philadelphia: Fortress Press, 1963.

Ellul, Jacques. *The Humiliation of the Word,* translated by Joyce Main Hanks. Grand Rapids: Eerdmans, 1981.

Feil, Ernst. *The Theology of Dietrich Bonhoeffer,* translated by Martin Rumscheidt. Philadelphia: Fortress Press, 1985.

Frye, Northrop. *The Great Code: Bible and Literature.* New York: Harcourt Brace Jovanovich, 1981.

Gremmels, C., and W. Huber, eds. *Theologie und Freundschaft; Wechselwirkungen: Eberhard Bethge und Dietrich Bonhoeffer* (Theology and friendship; interactions: Eberhard Bethge and Dietrich Bonhoeffer). Munich: Chr. Kaiser, 1994.

Gremmels, C., and H. Pfeiffer. *Theologie und Biographie: Zum Beispiel Dietrich Bonhoeffer* (Theology and biography: For example, Dietrich Bonhoeffer). Munich: Chr. Kaiser, 1983.

Grözinger, A. *Die Sprache des Menschen: Ein Handbuch; Grundwissen für Theologinnen und Theologen* (Human language: A manual; basic knowledge for theologians). Munich: Chr. Kaiser, 1991.

Heitink, Gerben. *Pastoraat als hulpverlening* (Pastoral care as giving help). Kampen: Kok, 1977.

Hoogstraten, Hans Dirk van. *Interpretatie: Een onderzoek naar de veranderingen in het denken van Dietrich Bonhoeffer en naar de consequenties daarvan voor de vertolking van de bijbel* (Interpretation: An inquiry into the changes in the thought of Dietrich Bonhoeffer and into their consequences for the interpretation of the Bible). Assen: Van Gorcum, 1973.

Huntemann, Georg. *The Other Bonhoeffer: An Evangelical Reassessment.* Translated by Todd Huizenga. Grand Rapids: Baker, 1993.

Jager, Okke. *Eigentijdse Verkondiging: Beschouwingen over de vertolking van het Evangelie in het taaleigen van de moderne mens* (Present-day proclamation: Reflections on the interpretation of the gospel in the idiom of modern humanity). Kampen: Kok, 1967.

———. *De verbeelding aan het woord: Pleidooi voor een dichterlijker en zakelijker spreken over God* (Imagination speaks: An argument for speaking more poetically and matter-of-factly about God). Baarn: Ten Have, 1988.

Jüngel, Eberhard. *God as the Mystery of the World: On the Foundation of the Theology of the Crucified One in the Dispute between Theism and Atheism*, translated by Darrell L. Guder. Grand Rapids: Eerdmans, 1983.

Klemperer, V. *LTI: Notizbuch eines Philologen* (LTI: Notebook of a philologist). Leipzig: Reclam, 1985.

Kodalle, K.-M. *Dietrich Bonhoeffer — Zur Kritik seiner Theologie* (Dietrich Bonhoeffer — a critique of his theology). Gütersloh: Gütersloher Verlag, 1991.

Kuhlmann, Helga. "Die Ethik Dietrich Bonhoeffers — Quelle oder Hemmschuh für feministisch-theologische Ethik?" (Dietrich Bonhoeffer's ethics: Source or hindrance for feminist-theological ethics?), *Zeitschrift für evangelische Ethik* 37/2 (1993) 106-20.

Lange, Ernst. *Chancen des Alltags: Überlegungen zur Funktion des christlichen Gottesdienstes in der Gegenwart* (Everyday chances: Reflections on the function of Christian worship today). Munich: Chr. Kaiser, 1984.

Lange, Frits de. *Grond onder de voeten: Burgerlijkheid bij Dietrich Bonhoeffer* (Ground under the feet: Bourgeois culture in Dietrich Bonhoeffer). Kampen: Kok, 1985.

Marsh, Charles. *Reclaiming Dietrich Bonhoeffer: The Promise of His Theology.* New York/Oxford: Oxford University Press, 1994.

Mayer, R., and P. Zimmerling. *Dietrich Bonhoeffer heute. Die Aktualität seines Lebens und Werk* (Dietrich Bonhoeffer Today. The actuality of his life and work). Giessen/Basel: Brunnen, 1992.

————. *Dietrich Bonhoeffer — Mensch hinter Mauern: Theologie und Spiritualität in den Gefängnisjahren* (Dietrich Bonhoeffer — man behind walls: Theology and spirituality during the years of imprisonment). Giessen/Basel: Brunnen, 1993.

Müller, Christine-Ruth. *Dietrich Bonhoeffers Kampf gegen die nationalsozialistische Verfolgung und Vernichtung der Juden: Bonhoeffers Haltung zur Judenfrage im Vergleich mit Stellungnahmen aus der evangelischen Kirche und Kreisen des deutschen Widerstandes* (Dietrich Bonhoeffer's struggle against the National Socialist persecution and extermination of the Jews: Bonhoeffer's attitude toward the Jewish question in comparison with positions in the Evangelical Church and circles of the German Resistance Movement). Munich: Chr. Kaiser, 1990.

Neher, André. *Exile of the Word: From the Silence of the Bible to the Silence of Auschwitz*, translated by David Maisel. Philadelphia: Jewish Publication Society, 1981.

Pejsa, Jane. *Matriarch of Conspiracy: Ruth von Kleist 1867-1945.* Minneapolis: Kenwood, 1991.

Pelican, H. R. *Die Frömmigkeit Dietrich Bonhoeffers: Äußerungen, Grundlinien, Entwicklung* (The spirituality of Dietrich Bonhoeffer: Expressions, patterns, development). Vienna: Herder, 1981.

Phillips, John A. *Christ for Us in the Theology of Dietrich Bonhoeffer.* New York: Harper & Row, 1967.

Ramsey, I. T. *Religious Language: An Empirical Placing of Theological Phrases.* London: SCM, 1957.

Rasmussen, Larry R. *Earth Community, Earth Ethics.* Maryknoll, N.Y.: Orbis, 1996.

Riesman, David. *The Lonely Crowd: A Study of the Changing American Character.* New Haven: Yale University Press, 1950.

Rohrbach, W. *Das Sprachdenken Rosenstock-Huessys* (Rosenstock-Huessy's thoughts on language). Stuttgart: Kohlhammer, 1973.

Searle, J. R. *Speech Acts: An Essay in the Philosophy of Language.* Cambridge: Cambridge University Press, 1969.

————. *Expression and Meaning: Studies in the Theory of Speech Acts.* Cambridge: Cambridge University Press, 1979.

Sperna Weiland, J. *Het einde van de religie: Verder op het spoor van Bonhoeffer* (The end of religion: Pursuing the path of Bonhoeffer). Baarn: Het Wereldvenster, 1970.

Staats, R. "Adolf von Harnack im Leben Dietrich Bonhoeffers" (Adolf von Harnack in the life of Dietrich Bonhoeffer), *Theologische Zeitschrift* 37/2 (1981) 94-121.

Strohm, C. *Theologische Ethik im Kampf gegen den Nationalsozialismus: Der Weg Dietrich Bonhoeffers mit den Juristen Hans van Dohnanyi und Gerhard Leibholz in den Widerstand* (Theological ethics in the struggle against National-Socialism: Dietrich Bonhoeffer's way with the jurists Hans von Dohnanyi and Gerhard Leibholz in the Resistance Movement). Munich: Chr. Kaiser, 1989.

Thurneysen, Eduard. "Der Aufgabe der Predigt" (The task of preaching) (1921), in *Aufgabe der Predigt* (The task of preaching), edited by G. Hummel, 105-18. Darmstadt: Wissenschaftliche Buchgesellschaft, 1971.

Tödt, H. E. "Dietrich Bonhoeffer's ökumenische Friedensethik" (Dietrich Bonhoeffer's ecumenical ethic of peace), in *Frieden — das unumgängliche Wagnis* (Peace — the inescapable venture). Internationales Bonhoeffer Forum 5. Munich: Chr. Kaiser, 1982.

Weder, H. *Neutestamentische Hermeneutik* (New Testament hermeneutics). Zurich: Theologischer Verlag, 1986.

Wendel, E. G. *Studien zur Homiletik Dietrich Bonhoeffers* (Studies on Dietrich Bonhoeffer's homiletics). Tübingen: Mohr (Siebeck), 1985.

Wiersinga, Herman. *Geloven bij daglicht: Verlies en toekomst van een traditie* (Believing by daylight: Loss and future of a tradition). Baarn: Ten Have, 1992.

Wittgenstein, Ludwig. *Tractatus Logico-philosophicus.* 1921. Reprint, London: Routledge & Kegan Paul, 1961.

———. *Philosophical Investigations,* translated by G. E. M. Anscombe. New York: Macmillan, 1958.

Wonneberger, R., and H. P. Hecht. *Verheißung und Versprechen: Eine theologische und sprachanalytische Klärung* (Promise and vow: A theological and linguistic analysis). Göttingen: Vandenhoeck & Ruprecht, 1986.

Zilleßen, D., ed. *Praktisch-theologische Hermeneutik* (Practical theological hermeneutics). Rheimbach-Merzbach: CMZ-Verlag, 1991.

Zimmermann, Wolf-Dieter. *Wir nannten ihn Bruder Bonhoeffer: Einblicke in ein hoffnungsvolles Leben* (We called him Brother Bonhoeffer: Insights into a hopeful life). Berlin: Wichern, 1995.

Zimmerman, Wolf-Dieter, and Ronald Gregor Smith, eds. *I Knew Dietrich Bonhoeffer,* translated by Käthe Gregor Smith. New York: Harper & Row, 1966.

Index